SERENA HOLDER

Cover design and interior layout by Derville Lowe

For further information, inquiries and orders contact the author:
Serena Holder-Campbell
Maryland, USA
Email: serenaholder@gmail.com

ISBN: 9798864696323

CONTENTS

LESSON ONE

Sex And Sexuality In Context:
A Delightful Landscape

Once upon a time, in two distant corners of the world, there lived two individuals, Lacey and Maxwell. They were both vibrant people and unapologetically, embraced their unique sexualities, and expressed them most delightfully, even though they were worlds apart. Lacey, a free-spirited artist, resided in a bohemian neighbourhood nestled in the heart of a bustling city. Her world was filled with vibrant colours, eccentric artwork, and a sense of liberation that echoed through her every brush stroke. Lacey's sexuality was integral to her being, and she navigated it with grace and confidence.

On the other hand, Maxwell lived in a small coastal town enveloped by the tranquil beauty of nature. He was a kindhearted writer, fascinated by the intricate dance between emotions and words. Maxwell's sexuality was like a gentle breeze, guiding him toward new experiences and connections that allowed him to explore himself more deeply.

Lacey's delightfully artistic expressions of love and sensuality can be seen in her paintings and sculptures. Every stroke of her brush, every curve of clay, conveyed a message of liberation and desire.

Her artwork captivated the hearts and minds of those who encountered it, evoking a sense of curiosity and awakening. With his poetic prowess, Maxwell weaved tales of passion and intimacy through his words. He wrote of love in myriad forms, capturing the essence of desire and connection. His stories transcended societal norms, inviting readers to embrace their unique expressions of sexuality without judgment.

Unbeknownst to Lacey and Maxwell, their paths were destined to cross one fateful summer. They found themselves attending an art exhibition in a picturesque coastal town. As they entered the gallery, their eyes met, and an instant connection sparked between them. Lacey admired Maxwell's eloquence, while Maxwell was captivated by Lacey's inhabited creativity. They spend hours exploring the exhibition, sharing their thoughts on art and life. Their conversations flowed effortlessly as if they had known each other forever.

Lacey invited Maxwell to her studio as the sun began to set, casting a golden glow over the horizon. Nestled amidst a lush garden, her sanctuary was a haven of artistic expression. Paintings adorned the walls, sculptures stood proudly, and the fragrant scent of creativity filled the air.

In this delightful landscape, Lacey and Maxwell embraced a journey of sensual exploration. They revelled in the beauty of touch, the symphony of breaths, and the harmony of their desires intertwining. Their lovemaking became an art form, a dance of passion and vulnerability, expressed with both tenderness and intensity.

Days turned into nights, nights into weeks, as Lacey and Maxwell continued exploring the depth of their desires. Their connection grew more pungent, fueled by trust and a shared understanding of the power of their sexuality. Together, they created a safe space where their fantasies could come to life and be their authentic selves without reservation. Their delightful journey continued beyond the walls of Lacey's studio. They ventured into the world, unafraid to express their love openly, challenging societal norms and inspiring others to embrace their unique sexualities. Lacey's paintings and Maxwell's stories gained a new dimension, influenced by the love they shared and the liberation they embodied.

Lacey and Maxwell lived their separate lives, forever connected by the delightful landscape they had discovered together. They taught the world that sexuality when expressed with authenticity and respect, could be a beautiful tapestry of passion, love, and self-discovery. Their legacy reminds us to embrace our unique sexualities and navigate the delightful landscape of desire with grace and joy.

Food For Thought:

Nowadays, discussions surrounding sex and sexuality have become increasingly prominent. Yet, many people do not understand their true meanings and develop many misconceptions concerning these two deeply human-affiliated concepts. As we strive for greater inclusivity and understanding, we must explore these topics in context, considering the historical, cultural, and social factors that shape our understanding of sex and sexuality.

Sexuality, as a multidimensional concept, encompasses a broad spectrum of identities, orientations, and expressions. Sexuality is not about who we have sex with or how often it is done. Sexuality is about sexual feelings, thoughts, attractions, and behaviours toward other people. It goes beyond the traditional boundary of male and female, heterosexual and homosexual. Additionally, it challenges us to recognize the diversity within human experiences. As we find other people physically, sexually, or emotionally attractive, we are essentially experiencing the expression of our sexuality. Sexuality is diverse and personal and a significant part of who we are. Discovering your sexuality can be a liberating, exciting, and positive experience.

Through Cultural And Sexual Eyes:

Culture has helped to shape our understanding of sex and sexuality. Each culture has rules, norms, taboos, and values influencing how individuals perceive and express their sexual desires. Cultural doctrine reminds us that what might be considered acceptable or normal in one culture may be viewed differently in another. Recognizing this cultural diversity helps advance compassion and understanding towards individuals from different backgrounds.

In recent years, society has witnessed significant progress in challenging societal norms and advocating for the rights and dignity of individuals across the spectrum of sexual orientations and gender identities. This significant progress has opened conversations about intersectionality, acknowledging that individuals may face multiple layers of discrimination based on their race, ethnicity, social class, or disability, in addition to their sexual orientation or gender identity.

This book, therefore, seeks to explore the varying types of relationships, perspectives around sexual advancements, and diverse perspectives that continue to dominate this modern era.

Exploring The Kaleidoscope Of Shapes In The World Of Sex:

Sexuality is complex and multifaceted, primarily since it encompasses the physical, emotional, and psychological dimensions. This complexity and multifaceted lens ignite the creation of a rich and diverse landscape understood through various shapes. The landscape of sex is a kaleidoscope of forms, each representing the varying aspects of human sexuality. Join in this journey to explore the landscapes of sex through the lens of a kaleidoscope, symbolizing the ever-changing, vibrant, and interconnected nature of the human sexual experience.

The Circle - Unity and Connection:

The circle represents the unity and connection that sex promotes between individuals. It symbolizes the coming together of two physical and emotional people seeking to create a bond of intimacy and trust. Like the circle, sex has no defined beginning or end but forms a continuous loop of pleasure, exploration, and penetrating connection.

The Triangle - Deep Desire, Intimacy, And Passion:

The triangle represents the three fundamental aspects of sex: desire, intimacy, and passion. Each side represents one of these dimensions, intersecting at the core of sexual experiences. Desire ignites the spark that gets fires of passion. Intimacy intertwines emotional closeness, and a strong, warm, firm bond and love fuel the intimate intensity of each delicious encounter. Together, these elements create a dynamic and fulfilling sexual panorama.

The Spiral - Growth And Evolution:

The spiral shape embodies the growth, evolution, and exploration that occur within the landscape of sex. Just as a spiral expands outward, sexual experiences can grow and develop over time. From discovering new desires and preferences to exploring different forms of pleasure, the spiral shape reflects the continuous journey of self-discovery and sexual growth.

The Puzzle - Compatibility And Communication:

The puzzle shape represents the importance of compatibility and communication in sexual relationships. Just as puzzle pieces fit together to form a complete picture, sexual partners must travel through and convey their desires, boundaries, and needs to ensure a harmonious experience. The puzzle shape emphasizes the significance of proper understanding, patience, tolerance, and shared discussion that creates a fulfilling sexual platform.

The Wave - Ebb And Flow:

The wave shape represents the urban flow of sexual experiences. It symbolizes the natural rhythms, highs, and lows in sexual relationships. Like waves crashing against the shore, sexual encounters can vary in intensity, frequency, and satisfaction. Recognizing the fluidity and understanding and embracing these fluctuations contribute to a healthier and more balanced sexual terrain.

From the unity and connection of the circle, sex is revealed. Love and excitement transcend through the desires, intimacy, and passions of the triangle. Growth and evolution, symbolized by the spiral, acknowledges constant change. The importance of compatibility and communication reflected in the puzzle gives credence to each voice. The ebon flow of sexual expression seen in the wave depicts personality.

These shapes offer a visual and conceptual framework to understand and appreciate the diverse dimensions of human sexuality. By exploring and embracing this landscape with qualities inclusive of empathy, respect, and open-mindedness, we can cultivate a more fulfilling and harmonious sexual journey for ourselves and the people with whom intimate lines cross.

LESSON TWO

Unlocking Fulfillment And Satisfaction In Marriage: A Guide To Lasting Happiness

Nathaniel and Alciann have been married for over eleven years. They met during their college years. From the moment their eyes met, there was an undeniable connection. As if the universe had conspired to bring them together, their love blossomed like a delicate flower, growing stronger daily. They were known far and wide for their radiant smiles, infectious laughter, and the unwavering joy that seemed to surround them. Their love story was a testament to their enduring bond and inspiration for those who crossed them.

Nathaniel and Alciann embarked on a beautiful journey filled with dreams, laughter, and shared adventures. Both Nathaniel and Alciann were passionate about exploring the world, immersing themselves in new cultures, and challenging the limits of their comfort zone. Together, they climbed mountains, hiked through vast forests, and sailed across oceans, creating memories that would last a lifetime. Their happiness went beyond grand adventures. Nathaniel and Alciann found joy in the simple things too. Whether it was cooking together, taking long walks hand in hand, or snuggling under a blanket on a rainy day, they cherished the moments that brought them closer.

Their secret to lasting happiness lay in their unwavering commitment to each other. They understood that a marriage thrived on trust, respect, and open, honest communication. They never let a day pass without expressing their love and gratitude for each other. Their love was a living, breathing entity nurtured by their shared dreams, mutual support, and unwavering loyalty. As the years passed, Nathaniel and Alciann decided to share their stories of lasting happiness with others. They started a blog named "Joyful Hearts," where they share their experiences, insights, and lessons learned from their journey together. Their words resonated with readers worldwide, touching hearts and inspiring others to cultivate joy in their relationships.

Nathaniel and Alciann hosted workshops and seminars, spreading their message of love, forgiveness, and gratitude. Couples who attended these events left with renewed hope and a deeper understanding of what it truly meant to find joy in their marriages. Nathaniel and Alciann's love story became a beacon of hope for those who believed that lasting happiness was possible. Through their blog, workshops, and personal interactions, they reminded others that they could find joy in everyday movements, the laughter shared over a meal, the general touch of a loved one, and the unconditional love that knows no bounds.

Their legacy as a couple who experienced genuine joy in their marriage grew with each passing day. They understood that happiness was not an end goal, but a continuous journey filled with ups and downs, triumphs, and challenges. Their unwavering commitment to nurturing their love and choosing joy in every circumstance set them apart. Each day, Nathaniel and Alciann's love story inspires countless couples, reminding them that true happiness lies not in the grand gestures but in the everyday choices they make to love and cherish each other. Their legacy will forever be etched in the hearts of those who believe in the power of love and the enduring joy it can bring.

Marriage is a sacred union that brings two individuals together in a lifelong commitment. It is a beautiful journey that requires significant effort, understanding, and continuous nurturing to achieve true fulfillment and satisfaction. This lesson will explore the key elements that contribute to a thriving, joyful, and fulfilling marriage.

The Foundation Of A Strong Marriage, The Art Of Communication:

In every aspect of life, for life to be productive and successful, it must incorporate open and honest communication. This open and honest communication is indicative of being the cornerstone of any successful marriage. Regularly expressing feelings, thoughts, and desires to loved ones is necessary. Actively listening to their needs, as well, is the first place to start the communication process. Effective communication fosters understanding, trust, and a deeper emotional connection that leads to greater satisfaction in the relationship.

Cultivate Emotional Intimacy:

Most people fail to understand that emotional intimacy goes beyond physical closeness. It encompasses sharing vulnerabilities, which people frequently fail to allow to be seen. Most often seen in sharing dreams and fears with partners. Emotional intimacy involves creating a safe space for both individuals to be authentic behind closed doors. Prioritizing quality time, and engaging in meaningful conversations, contribute holistically to emotional intimacy. Empathy and support are also vital when nurturing emotional intimacy and strengthening the bond between spouses. It also enhances their overall satisfaction with that relationship.

Mutual Respect And Appreciation:

Respect and appreciation are fundamental to a healthy, productive marriage. That is why it is so relevant to acknowledge and value partners' opinions, efforts, and accomplishments. The very expression of gratitude for the little things they do and never take for granted should go beyond any boundaries. By cultivating respect and appreciation, you create an atmosphere of love, validation, and happiness in your relationship.

Our Role In Compromise And Flexibility:

Compromise is essential in any partnership. You and your partner must be unique individuals with different perspectives, needs, and desires. As such, people must learn to find common ground, seek solutions that satisfy both parties and be willing to adapt to circumstances that require change. By embracing compromise and flexibility, you promote harmony and reduce conflicts while fostering a more satisfying marriage.

Growing With The Right Support:

In any marriage situation, participants should seek to encourage personal growth and support each other's ambitions and aspirations. It needs continuous celebration of each other's successes and providing a nurturing environment for self-improvement. By fostering individual growth, you create a stronger foundation for the marriage to work, allowing both partners to flourish and find fulfillment within themselves and the boundaries of the relationship.

Quality Time And Shared Experiences:

Many individuals within relationships do not thrive because they fail to be available for each other and prioritize being together to have shared experiences. Engaging in activities both partners enjoy, whether trying new hobbies, travelling, or simply spending quality time at home, plays an important role. Creating positive memories and shared adventures is essential since it strengthens the bond and creates a sense of fulfillment and satisfaction in marriages.

Forgiveness And Letting Go Of Resentment:

Indeed, no marriage is perfect, and conflicts are inevitable. An important lesson is to learn to forgive, let go of resentment, and work through disputes with patience and understanding. Without tolerance, people continue to hold on to grudges that only create toxicity and hinder the growth and happiness of the relationship. The Bible speaks powerfully about forgiveness, allowing great healing of the mind and soul and paving the way for a stronger, more fulfilling bond.

A fulfilling and satisfying marriage is a journey that requires commitment and effort. Active participation from both partners is necessary to make it work and bring the joy and satisfaction that each person requires. You can create a strong and joyful partnership by cultivating enriched communication of each other's needs in emotional intimacy, respect, and appreciation and embracing compromise and personal growth. Remember, a happy marriage is not a destination. Instead, it is a continuous process of nurturing and cherishing each other, which leads to a fulfilling lifetime.

LESSON THREE

Rediscovering Intimacy: Navigating Sex In Marriage In The Modern Age

Sophia and Daniel had lived together for many years and had built a strong foundation of love and companionship. However, as time passed, they faced a challenge that threatened to tear them apart as they navigated their intimate life. Sophia and Daniel had always believed that a healthy physical connection was essential to their marriage. However, after years of monotony and familiarity, their once passionate encounters had become routine and predictable. The situation led to a growing sense of dissatisfaction and frustration, causing a strain on their relationship.

One evening, as they sat on their porch, sipping tea and watching the sunset, Sophia broke the silence. "Daniel, I've been feeling disconnected from you lately. Our lovemaking has lost its spark, and I yearn for that connection we used to have." Daniel looked at Sophia, his eyes filled with concern. "I feel the same, Sophia. But I do not know how to fix it. I don't want to lose you, but we've exhausted all our options." Determined not to give up, Sofia suggested seeking guidance from a professional. They booked an appointment with a renowned therapist who specialized in marital intimacy. The therapist encourages them to open up about their desires, fears, and vulnerabilities during their sessions.

As Sophia and Daniel delved deep into their thoughts and emotions, they realized that their struggles in the bedroom were not solely physical but about emotional connection. They have grown distant, focusing on their individual needs rather than nurturing their bond as a couple. The therapist suggested a path of discovery, urging them to create new experiences together.

Sofia and Daniel decided to embark on a journey of exploration, both inside and outside the bedroom. They started by reconnecting on an emotional level. They set aside time daily to talk and truly listen to one another. They share their dreams, fears, and fantasies, allowing vulnerability and trust to flourish.

They decided to try new things to ignite the passion in their intimate life. They embarked on a quest to explore different techniques and positions and even introduce toys into their bedroom. They let go of inhibitions and embrace the adventures of discovering each other's desires. Their journey did not end there.

Sophia and Daniel realized that intimacy extended beyond the physical realms. They learned the importance of non-sexual touch, such as holding hands, cuddling, and gentle caresses.

These simple gestures reignited the flame of love and helped them feel connected even outside the bedroom.

Sophia and Daniel witnessed a beautiful transformation in their marriage as the days turned into weeks and weeks into months. They were both fearful that the love, passion, and connection between them were lost but, instead, rekindled with newfound intensity. Their experience taught them that intimacy was not a static state but a continuous journey. It required effort, communication, and a willingness to evolve together. They understood that intimacy was not solely about sex but about fostering a deep emotional bond that transcends physicality.

Sophia and Daniel's renowned love and passion inspired all who heard of it or knew where their life was heading. They began sharing their story, hoping to help couples who faced similar challenges. They believed that any team could overcome obstacles and reclaim the joy and intimacy they desire with perseverance and a commitment to growth.

And so, Sophia and Daniel's love story became a beacon of hope, reminding everyone that even in the face of adversity, love could conquer all, and the journey of rediscovering intimacy was worth taking.

One crucial aspect of the sacred union is sexual intimacy, which plays a significant role in maintaining a healthy and fulfilling relationship. However, in the modern age, with its fast-paced lifestyle and ever-evolving societal norms, couples often find it challenging to prioritize and navigate their sexual lives effectively. This lesson explores the importance of sex in marriage, the common challenges teams face, and strategies to maintain a satisfying sexual connection in the modern era.

The Importance Of Sexual Intimacy In Marriage

Sexual intimacy in marriage goes beyond physical pleasure; it strengthens emotional bonds, fosters trust, and enhances overall relationship satisfaction. Regular sexual activity increases happiness, reduces stress, and improves partner communication. It serves as a unique expression of love and desire, allowing couples to connect on a deeper level, both physically and emotionally.

Challenges In The Modern Age Marriage

No relationship can guarantee that challenges will not occur, even with your best efforts. In this modern age, marriages face many challenges that may be unique. First of all, people struggle to accept and be alone with themselves on any given day. It won't be easy to be with anyone, even for a day. Indeed, it is easy to see how every relationship can be threatened or challenged in some way or the other. We should examine these potentially threatening circumstances where and what may arise as challenges.

1. **Busy schedules**: Many couples in this era lead busy lives, juggling demanding careers that require long hours and sometimes expensive travel. Coupled with the demands of work, children, and other responsibilities, they often leave little time for couples to prioritize their sexual relationships. Work-life balance has never been a secret to impacting marriages. It often leaves little or no time and energy for intimacy, leading to a decline in sexual frequency and satisfaction. Balancing work life can cause strains on marriages, leading to feelings of neglect and resentment. For many relationships, the participants never recover from these woes and eventually settle on separation as the acceptable solution.

2. **Technological distractions:** While in other sections of this book, the use of technology presents positives for relationships, it is still a concern that the digital age has brought with it an array of distractions that can hinder intimacy, such as excessive screen time, social media, and the constant availability of entertainment. With the advent of smartphones and their constant connectivity, couples too often find themselves engrossed in these niceties and essentially neglect each other. The result of this is a decrease in sexual connection.

3. **Body image and self-esteem issues:** The pervasiveness of realistic beauty standards, as portrayed in the media, can lead to insecurities and negative body image, affecting one's confidence and willingness to engage in sexual activities.

4. **Change in family dynamics:** In this modern era, family dynamics have changed drastically to include blended families, stepchildren, and significant differences in cultural backgrounds. Steering through all these dynamics where there might be differences in opinions and expectations from external family members can cause considerable strains on couples.

5. **Social pressures and comparisons**: Societal expectations, now twined with social media, have a way of placing undue stress on marriages. Couples too often compare their relationships and partners to what they see glamorized on social media. When this occurs, individuals are left feeling inadequate or discontent.

6. **Stress and Fatigue:** Life these days tends to be associated with high stress and fatigue levels. Without adequate coping skills, couples are highly likely to experience distress in mustering sexual desires and performance. This issue ultimately will result in low libido and unfulfilling sex life.

7. **Medical conditions and hormonal imbalances:** Contrary to popular beliefs, both men and women face the challenge of

hormonal imbalances. Menopause in women and andropause in men affects couples facing middle ages. Both conditions do impact sexual performance or just the urge to engage in the act of intimacy. Chronic medical conditions, such as diabetes, affect couples' libido or sexual functioning. Often, it is just the consumption of certain medications that impedes functioning. Often enough, people will also sacrifice their health and well-being by stopping their medications to not give up on sex. The strain on the relationship will be evident whichever way this plays out.

8. **Monotony and lack of novelty**: For many couples, not restricted by any specific issue, overtime falls into a routine leading to a lack of originality, excitement, and joy in the bedroom. Without being spontaneous and creating intimate appeal, the risk of that relationship failing is high. These are the times when engaging in infidelity and extramarital affairs is much easier. When such a thing as boredom enters the marriage, many find it more appealing to just seek satisfaction elsewhere. Without conscious effort and awareness, a union goes adrift before intervention arrives. In these trying times, it has become essential for couples to recognize and address these challenges openly and honestly.

Reading books and participating in couples' conferences, seminars, podcasts, and reading literature addressing marriage challenges help lighten the burdens experienced and other unforeseen issues. One must, however, recognize that with professional help, a therapist can restore relationships before they get to the level of disrepair. A professional counsellor can provide guidance and support to navigate this whole landscape of the sexual aspects of marriage.

Strategies For Maintaining A Satisfying Sexual Connection

Maintaining a satisfying sexual connection requires creative strategies to be developed and implemented. It is always good to feel deeply linked to our partner; therefore, the effort one puts in should reflect the same. The first and maybe most important step is an open, frank discussion. In many relationships, there are no discussions of the desires, fantasies, or needs of partners. Many, while they have personal preferences, never choose to express them. They rely on their partners to explore possibilities, and it becomes overly frustrating without their met needs because of poor communication. Complete fulfillment of a sexual nature requires the discussion of where and how each partner, more so women, desires to be touched. The deep fantasies, such as threesome or multiple partners; oral and anal sex, are just a few expressed.

For many, these are just fantasies, yet harbour the wish to explore them. Discussing these and other desires, dreams, and concerns is only necessary to understand each other's needs and preserve a healthy sexual bond. Honest conversations can help address any underlying issues and foster a strong foundation of trust.

Prioritizing quality time is another component of building strategies for maintaining a satisfying sexual connection. It is prudent to ascribe dedicated time for each other, free from distractions, to connect and engage in activities that promote emotional and physical intimacy. The simple planning and execution of date nights, weekend getaways, or simply getting time for uninterrupted conversations can prove adequate.

The third recommended strategy for maintaining a satisfying sexual connection is mindfully embracing technology. While technology can be a distraction, it enhances intimacy—enhanced intimacy through the exploration of apps, books, or educational resources designed to improve sexual knowledge. The debate continues regarding the open option of pornography as an intruder in relationships versus being an enhancement and enrichment in sexual intimacy. When used with this intention, there will be the where-with-all to improve communication and experimentation within the boundaries of the relationship.

The following strategy for maintaining a satisfying sexual connection is self-care and body positivity. When you prioritize self-care, a positive self-image boosts confidence and self-esteem. As such, it is also wise to encourage partners to do the same, celebrating and appreciating each other's bodies and uniqueness. Sadly, many people in intimate relationships have never seen their partner's body or anatomy out of clothes. Every private act occurs either in the dead of night or fully clothed for fear of discomfort or insecurities.

Another strategy for maintaining a satisfying sexual connection is to seek professional help. As one aims to keep the relationship spirited and happy, there comes a time when people must recognize that even with our best efforts, we need professionals' help. If challenges linger or become overwhelming, seeking guidance from a licensed therapist or sexologist can be beneficial. These professionals can provide valuable insights, tools, and exercises tailored to your needs while helping you navigate roadblocks and rejuvenate your sexual connection.

What are the core messages in this lesson? Sexual intimacy is a vital component of fulfilling and happy marriages and, therefore, requires effort and attention in this new era. By prioritizing rich discussion regarding nurturing a solid and satisfying sexual connection, quality time spent in partnership, and self-care, couples can overcome the challenges they face.

Remember, each relationship is unique, with no one-size-fits-all situations or solutions. Begin to embrace the journey together. As you do so, grasp the skills and willingness to endure. By committing to maintaining a healthy sexual bond, couples can rediscover the joy and fulfillment of intimacy in marriage.

LESSON FOUR

Exploring Pleasures: Modern Society And The Art Of Sexual Positions

Cole and Nikisha have been a couple for several years. They were both adventurous people who sought to explore the world around them but also their pleasures, desires, and passions. Their love was deep and steamy as they embarked on many journeys of lust, discovering the art of lovemaking utilizing various sex positions.

They love to explore new styles of intimacy and creatively indulge in porn to increase their world of excitement. Nikisha, with her fiery red hair and mesmerizing green eyes, possessed an insatiable curiosity when it came to matters of pleasure. On the other hand, Cole was a gentle and skilled lover who was always eager to indulge in his beloved Nikisha's desires. Together, they created a safe space to explore their most intimate fantasies.

Nikisha and Cole shared many intimate moonlight nights as the stars twinkled above, designing deep, penetrating sexual ecstasy. That night they decided to start their sensual exploration and cuddled in a deep embrace with tongue-trusted back and forth in each other's mouths. Cole rubbed his naked skin against Nikisha's stiff tits that stood erect, yearning for Cole's tongue; the room steamed with yearning. Before long, they became so aroused with passion that she took charge of her hunger, and he claimed her under the welcoming classic cowgirl position.

Nikisha straddled Cole, her delicate hands finding support on his chest. As she moved gracefully, their bodies merged into a harmonious rhythm, their connection deepening with every motion. This position allowed Cole to take control, and Cole revelled in the sensation of surrendering to her desire.

Feeling empowered by the first round of their adventure, Nikisha suggested they try the reverse cowgirl position. With a mischievous smile, she turned around, facing away from Cole, who lay on his back awaiting the thrilling delight. As she rode him, their passion and intensity grew as if they were discovering a whole new level of ecstasy. This position allowed Cole to appreciate the captivating view of Nikisha's curves while Nikisha relished the freedom to explore her pleasures. Eager to add a twist to their sensual repertoire, Cole flipped her sharply to try a modified version of the missionary position. He placed a pillow under Nikisha's hips and lifted her legs, creating a new angle that allowed her deeper penetration. As they gazed into each other's eyes, their passion intensified, and the connection between their souls became inseparable from their physical union.

Their exploration continued, and one evening as they felt a deep longing for each other's soul to become one, Nikisha playfully took her red thong off and mounted up on all fours and, with a draws-less ass, crawled on the carpet of their fabulous bedroom. Cole gazed at her longingly as a dog happy with his master, ready to embrace a session in the doggy-style position. She arched her back invitingly with her hands and knees resting on the floor. Captivated by her alluring stance, Cole entered her from behind, while they both revelled in the primal pleasure that this position offered. Their bodies moved in unison, a dance of raw desire, as they surrendered to the animalistic urge that consumed them.

As their journey of passion progressed, Nikisha longed for a moment of tenderness and closeness. One night, she curled up on her side, pulled Cole close, and they embraced the spooning position. Their bodies fit perfectly together, and they revelled in this position's intimate connection. It spoke of trust, love, and an unbreakable bond, reminding them that passion can be gentle and nurturing too.

Through their exploration of these various sex positions, Nikisha and Cole discovered greater pleasure and a deeper understanding of their desire and one another. Their love grew stronger with every shared experience as they celebrated their bodies and the great union they created. It is essential to know that the experiences shared by

Nikisha, and Cole were consensual and born out of deep trust and mutual respect.

Exploring sex positions can allow couples to find new dimensions of pleasure and intimacy, but it is crucial to prioritize communication and consent in any sexual encounter.

And so, Nikisha and Cole continue their passionate journey, embracing new positions and scenarios as they continue to educate themselves about the vast world of pleasure. Their love story became a testament to the power of exploration, communication, and understanding in matters of the heart and desire.

Sexuality is a fundamental aspect of human life, and throughout history, individuals have embraced the myriad of sexual positions to enhance pleasure and deep intimate connections. In today's modern society, exploring sexual positions has expanded, allowing individuals to discover new ways to experience joy. This lesson discusses several sex positions that can bring pleasure and intimacy to couples in contemporary times.

Missionary With A Twist

A missionary with a twist refers to a variation of the traditional sexual position known as the missionary. The missionary position means that the person penetrating, whether with a penis or a strap-on, is on top, and the person receiving is lying underneath them. This position, unlike doggy style and others, requires both persons to face each other, allowing for eye contact and kissing during these pleasurable moments. This position also provides for kissing of the breasts and nipples, which are two of our most significant erogenous zones.

This specific twist can vary depending on personal preferences and creativity but generally involves modifications of body angle movements or incorporating additional props. The classic missionary position remains popular due to its intimacy and eye contact. However, modern variations can heighten pleasure. Elevating the woman's legs, using pillows or props, can increase the angle of penetration, stimulating deeper vaginal and G-spot sensations for enhanced pleasure.

Doggy Style

Doggy style is a sex position in which the person penetrating stands or kneels behind their partner and inserts the penis or sex toy either in the vagina or anus. The classic doggy style, however, is when the person receiving is on all fours. Nonetheless, there have been variations to this position to add more pleasure and stimulation. Add description has long been celebrated for its primal nature and deep penetration. In modern times, couples can explore variations to intensify pleasure. The receiver can experiment with changing angles by arching their back or incorporating a pillow under their hips, leading to heightened sensation and increased clitoral stimulation. It simply takes some adjustments to find the most comfortable position.

Cowgirl

The cowgirl position entails the penetrating partner lying on his back with the other person sitting on top facing them in a squat on-top position. The female who is the receiving partner is in a kneeling position on top, pushing off the partner's chest and sliding up and down his thighs. The partner on top can vary in position to explore varying sensations.

In modern society, couples can enhance pleasure by experimenting with different angles and variations. For instance, the woman can lean forward or backward, allowing for a range of sensations while providing easy access to stimulating erogenous zones such as the clitoris.

The cowgirl position empowers the female or receiving partner to take control, dictating the pace and depth of the penetration and choice of angling of the body. This position also allows you to use vaginal and clitoral stimulation to your advantage. This position is suitable for persons with challenges having an orgasm due to the friction to the clitoris.

Reverse Cowgirl

The reverse cowgirl position entails the penetrating partner lying on his back with the other person sitting on top, facing away from them in a squat-on-top position. The female who is the receiving partner is kneeling on top, balancing by hugging the partner's upward-positioned knees and sliding up and down his thighs. This position offers a fresh perspective and can be pleasurable for both partners. The visual aspect allows for a unique angle of penetration, and the receiver can control the depth and pace of trust. Couples can experiment further by incorporating additional stimulation, such as manual play or sex toys, to intensify pleasure.

Spooning

Spooning is a position where both partners lie down on the same side, facing the same way. The masculine spoon, the penetrating partner, envelopes the receiving partner in a bear hug, tucking the knees behind. Spooning is an intimate position that allows for deeper connection and relaxed pleasure. In modern society, couples can incorporate additional stimulation by reaching around to massage the clitoris or stimulate the nipples, getting a heightened sense of satisfaction and intimacy.

The Butterfly

The butterfly sex position is much like the classic missionary except with some modifications. To get into that position, the receiving partner lies down on their back, on a flat surface such as a table or a bed, and their butt in the air with legs open and knees bent. The giver partner stands at the end of the surface you use, a table or bed, to penetrate the receiving partner with his penis or other sex toys. The receiving partner can either have the legs spread apart straight up in a "V" or rest their ankles on their partner's shoulders. With the receiver line on the edge of a bed or table, the giver can access various erogenous zones while providing intense pleasure. This position allows for deep penetration, clitoris stimulation, and easy access for manual play, making it a versatile choice for couples.

In modern society, exploring sexual positions has expanded, offering individuals and couples many options to enhance pleasure and intimacy. The possibilities are endless, from classic positions with modern twists to innovative variations. When exploring these positions, it is crucial to prioritize open communication, consent, and mutual pleasure. These factors are to ensure a safe and enjoyable experience for all involved. Remember, pleasure is subjective, and what matters most is finding what works best for you and your partner, creating a fulfilling and satisfying sexual journey.

LESSON FIVE

The Right Strategy To Attract A Suitable Partner: Building A Strong Foundation For Love

There was once a woman named Brianna who was determined to find true love. She had spent several years searching for a suitable partner, but all her previous relationships had ended in disappointment. Determined to break this pattern, Brianna decided to take a different approach. Brianna was a strategic thinker, believing that finding love required careful planning, just like any other important endeavour in life. She knew she had to design the right strategy to attract a partner who would perfectly match her. So, she settled on a journey of self-discovery and personal growth.

Brianna began to reflect on her desires, values, and her goals. She recognized that to attract a suitable partner, she needed first to become the best version of herself. Brianna started investing time in her hobbies and interests, nurturing her talents, and pursuing her passions. Brianna knew that loving herself was crucial before she could expect someone else to love her. Brianna's second step was to educate herself on building a solid foundation for love. She read books, watched YouTube videos on self-love, relationship building, values, and attitudes, and sought advice from experts specializing in healthy relationships.

Armed with newfound knowledge, Brianna was ready to implement her strategy. She started by being intentional about the people she surrounded herself with. Brianna sought out individuals who shared her values and aspirations. She joined clubs and organizations where she could meet like-minded individuals, expanding her social circle. This action allowed her to meet people who aligned with her goals and vision for the type of future she was looking for.

Brianna also became more mindful of her actions and behaviours. She improved her communication skills, learning to express her emotions effectively and listen attentively. She understood that a strong foundation for love required open, honest communication, and she prioritized it in her interactions with others.

As Brianna's confidence grew, she became more selective in her dating choices. She knew that compatibility was vital, so she didn't settle for less. She sought someone who shared her values, respected her boundaries, and supported her dreams. She believed that love was a partnership built on mutual respect and understanding.

Finally, after months of self-reflection and personal growth, Brianna met Michael. He was everything she had ever hoped for: kind, compassionate, and driven. They shared similar goals and values, and they effortlessly communicated and connected. Their relationship grew as they understood the importance of building a solid foundation. They worked on trust, honesty, and vulnerability, knowing these qualities were vital for lasting love.

Brianna and Michael supported and encouraged each other, remembering to celebrate their achievements and shared ones. As the years passed, Brianna and Michael's love continued to flourish. Their strong foundation had weathered the storms of life and, with their commitment to each other, had survived. Their love was a testament to Brianna's strategic approach to finding a suitable partner and building a solid foundation for love. Ultimately, Brianna's journey taught her that finding true love required more than chance or luck. It demanded self-reflection, commitment, personal growth, and a well-designed strategy. She realized that when she invested in herself and took deliberate actions, she attracted a genuinely compatible partner and was ready to build a lifetime of love.

Finding a suitable partner is a desire that many people hold dear and spend most of their lives trying to accomplish. However, achieving this goal requires more than just mere luck or chance encounters. Instead, it requires an excellent strategy that involves serious considerations. The consideration includes someone whose values align with yours and who shares the same or similar values, interests, and life goals. The differing elements will likely create significant challenges when these core components are opposite.

Notwithstanding that, there is the belief that the opposite attracts. If the negatives are way off, proceeding with such a relationship is a deterrent. However, following the right strategy increases the chance of building a solid foundation for an ever-fulfilling and satisfying relationship.

Here are some essential steps as you seek to create the right strategy to attract a suitable partner to build a strong foundation for love.

1. **Self-Reflection and Improvement:** As you embark on the journey toward finding a suitable partner, it is essential to reflect on your values, goals, and aspirations. Here is where you take the time to understand yourself better, identify your strengths and weaknesses, and work on your personal growth and development. By becoming the best version of yourself, ideally, you naturally attract individuals who will also appreciate and resonate with your authentic, beautiful self.

2. **Define What Your Ideal Partner Looks Like:** Having a clear picture of the qualities and different characteristics you would want in your partner is vital. At this stage, detailing is a crucial part of your journey, and therefore, you need to take the time to write down the main qualities and values you would need in your partner. These characteristics will examine qualities such as values, kindness, intelligence, ambition, and even a sense of

humour. While you must be realistic and practical, you must also be open-minded, recognizing that no one is perfect. Still, there are so many important traits that are non-negotiable for a healthy and compatible relationship.

3. **Nurture Your Social Circles:** An essential part of nurturing your social circles includes building a strong network of friends and acquaintances that can significantly expand your chances of meeting someone suitable. As you seek to grow and nurture your network, try to engage in activities and hobbies in which you are interested. These could include but are not limited to joining certain clubs, being a part of some organizations, attending and engaging in social events that you feel are critical for your development, and considering participating in online communities such as dating apps and others that cater to your specific interests. By surrounding yourself with like-minded individuals, you will likely find someone who shares your passions, dreams, and aspirations.

4. **Be Spontaneous And Be Ready For New Experiences:** When seeking to attract a suitable partner, stepping out of your comfort zone and being open to new experiences is essential. As you chart your way through new and varied settings, be prepared to embrace the opportunities as you try new stuff, explore various environments, and meet diverse people. These actions make you

more attractive, broaden your horizons, and increase your chances of finding someone who complements your lifestyle and interests.

5. **Cultivate A Positive Mindset:** Finding the right partner requires changing your mindset and adopting a more positive and confident persona. Positivity and confidence are attractive qualities that can significantly enhance your chances of attracting the right partner. You must focus on self-love, practice self-care, and seize every moment to maintain a positive outlook on life. By radiating positivity, you become more attractive in the eyes of the beholder and draw others towards you.

6. **Effective Communication:** The emphasis on communication transcends all points raised throughout this book. With much enthusiasm, this point reiterates that you become a superhuman when you develop a strong sense of touch and grasp the necessary skills. Cultivating the art of being an active listener enables you to express your thoughts and feelings honestly and to be receptive to your partner's perspectives. This active listening creates a solid foundation for understanding, trust, and emotional connection with potential partners.

7. **Patience And Perseverance:** There is this saying that patience is a virtue, and thus, when you are seeking to attract a suitable partner, you must recognize that it takes time. Therefore,

remaining patient and only settling for what you deserve is essential. It would help if you remembered that it is better to be alone than in a relationship that doesn't align with your values and goals. Thus, stay true to yourself and trust that the right person will come into your life when the timing is right. So, you have to be in this for the long haul.

Attracting a suitable partner requires a strategic approach rather than just a swift action. This strategic approach must involve self-reflection. Self-reflection helps to define who you are and what your life needs. It will also help to determine what an ideal partner looks like for you. An important goal is to nurture your social circles and be open to new experiences. Additionally, be prepared to develop a positive mindset and improve your communication skills while practicing tolerance and patience.

By following these steps, you will increase your chances of building a solid foundation for a loving and fulfilling relationship. Remember that finding the right partner is not an exact science. Instead, by implementing these strategies, you will set yourself on a path to attracting someone who is genuinely compatible and brings out your best version.

LESSON SIX

The Empowered Role Of Women In Sexual Intimacy For Modern Society

In a quiet town nestled by the sea lived a woman named Camilla. Camilla was a confident, intelligent, and independent, unafraid to embrace her desires and needs. Camilla knew that sexual intimacy was an essential part of her relationships, and she believed that taking the lead role could lead to a deeper connection with her partner. Camilla believed in the power of sexual intimacy and the importance of communication between partners. Determined to explore her needs and take the lead role, she embarked on a journey that would forever change her life and that of her partner, Warren.

Camilla's partner, Warren, was a kindhearted and considerate man who cherished their relationship. He admired her strength and was willing to follow her lead in their intimate moments. Although he had always been the one to take charge, he found himself intrigued and excited by the idea of Camilla guiding him through their shared passions.

Camilla and Warren were deeply in love. Their connection went beyond the physical, but Camilla yearned to strengthen their bond even further. She longed to take charge, to guide Warren through her desires, and to create an environment where both of their needs were met.

One evening, as the moon hung high in the sky, casting her gentle glow through the bedroom window, Camilla decided it was time to initiate her plan. She prepared an intimate setting in their bedroom, adorning it with soft candlelight and silk sheets that invited pleasure and exploration. With her heart racing, she nervously awaited Warren's arrival.

As Warren entered the room, he received a sigh that took his breath away. Camilla stood confidently, her eyes sparkling with anticipation. She took his hand and guided him towards the bed, whispering in his ears, "Tonight, my love, I want to lead us on a journey of pleasure where we both find fulfillment and satisfaction."

She was intrigued and open-minded; Warren nodded, placing his trust in Camilla's capable hands. She began by slowly undressing him, her hands gliding over his skin, exploring every inch of his body. With each touch, Camilla discovered what excited him, what made him shudder with pleasure. She listened to his moans and gasps, using them as a road map to his desires.

Camilla was not only focused on her partner's satisfaction but also on her own. She communicated her needs clearly, guiding Warren to explore her body in ways they had never experienced before. She encouraged him to discover the intricacies of her desires, showing him the power of vulnerability and trust.

Together, Camilla and Warren embarked on a journey of exploration guided by her lead. They tried new positions, experimented with different sensations, and discovered hidden depths of pleasure. Camilla's confidence in her desires became contagious, empowering Warren to communicate his needs openly.

Through their shared experiences, they learned to trust each other implicitly, creating a safe space to express their desires without judgment. It wasn't always easy, but they navigated challenges with open hearts and minds. Camilla's guidance instilled a sense of fulfillment in Warren, knowing he was satisfying her needs while experimenting and experiencing his pleasure. As time passed, Camilla and Warren continued to explore their desires together, their intimacy growing more profound. They became a testament to the power of communication, trust, and the beauty of a woman taking the lead.

In a world that often dictates rigid gender roles, Camilla defied societal expectations, proving that sexual empowerment and satisfaction were not limited to any one gender. She showed true intimacy blossomed in both partners, who felt heard, desired, and fulfilled. Camilla's journey transformed her life and left an indelible mark on her wonderful masculine man, Warren. They became partners who embraced their desires with open hearts, free from the constraints of societal norms. Together, they created a love story that celebrated the beauty of a woman taking the lead and left an inspiring legacy for others to pick up the trail and follow suit.

The role of women in sexual intimacy in recent times has seen a significant shift whereby women have undertaken a balance in sexual autonomy. As sexual intimacy is an unbroken part of human nature and plays a dynamic role in shaping our relationships and overall well-being, a crucial balance was necessary to add even greater value and equality. In recent years, there has been a significant shift in societal attitudes towards female sexuality and a more empowered role for women in sexual intimacy. This lesson aims to explore the evolving perceptions, challenges, and contributions of women in modern society regarding sexual intimacy.

From Breaking Stereotypes To Empowerment

Historically, societal norms and double standards often overshadow women's sexuality. However, in the present era, women are breaking free from these constraints and embracing their sexual desires and preferences. The liberation movement has paved the way for discussions about consent, pleasure, and self-expression, highlighting the importance of women's agency in sexual intimacy. One significant aspect of the evolving role of women in sexual intimacy is that they are reclaiming their sexual autonomy. Women are increasingly asserting their needs and desires, ensuring their voices are heard and respected. The evidence of this shift is seen and felt in more open conversations and greater equality in sexual relationships.

The Role of Education And Communication

The decisive role that education plays in enabling women to make informed decisions about their sexual lives, many take for granted. Modern society has witnessed a surge in sex education and awareness campaigns that aim to provide accurate information about sexual health, consent, and pleasure fundamentals. We have flogged this horse, so to speak, throughout this book, reinforcing that with improved knowledge, women are better equipped to communicate their desires, negotiate boundaries, and engage in fulfilling sexual relationships.

Women's Arena To Confront Taboos And Stigmas

Concerning the role of women in sexual intimacy in modern times, society's taboos and stigmas have long hindered open discussions and exploration. However, women have become braver and have started challenging the status quo of these social constructs and demanding a more inclusive and compassionate understanding of sexual intimacy. By speaking out against slut-shaming, body shaming, and other forms of judgment, women are creating an environment that embraces sexual diversity and celebrates individual choices. These strides, however, can only be seen in societies with monogamy.

Embracing Sexual Pleasure

Traditionally, discussions around sexual pleasure have been focused solely on male satisfaction, neglecting the needs and desires of women. However, women were not actively seeking and prioritizing their happiness, leading to a more fulfilling and balanced sexual experience. Instead, they left everything in the capable hands of the men, or so they thought! The acknowledgment of the female orgasm as an essential aspect of sexual intimacy has brought on a greater sense of equality and satisfaction for women. The evolving role of women in sexual intimacy in modern society is a testament to the progress towards gender equality and empowerment. Women are reclaiming their sexual autonomy, challenging societal norms, and embracing their desires and pleasures. As we continue to break down barriers, educate, and communicate, the role of women in sexual intimacy will undoubtedly continue to advance, increasing healthier and more fulfilling experiences for all.

LESSON SEVEN

The Role Of Men In Sexual Intimacy For Modern Society

Franco and Cassandra were a delighted and deeply connected couple. In the past, they did not have their relationship built on love, trust, and understanding of each other's desires and boundaries. Cassandra was a woman of a quiet spirit, and Franco was constantly the dominant partner in the relationship. They have had many disagreements, as he often felt that only he could determine when and how lovemaking occurs. Cassandra had little control over her wish for pleasure and only had a say if Franco was too tired to decide.

After years of ups and downs in the relationship, Cassandra confronted Franco one day and, without qualms, informed him that if they did not seek professional help, she was walking out the door, never to return. Since then, things changed for the better, and they got to a place where balance was evident. They had redefined traditional gender roles, embracing a dynamic that allowed them to explore their sexuality in an authentic and empowering way. In their intimate moments, Franco and Cassandra had created a safe space where they could express their desires and let go of societal pressures. Each encounter was a playground of mutual exploration, with the lines of traditional gender roles blurred, and they revelled in the freedom to be themselves.

One evening, as the sun dipped below the horizon, Cassandra and Franco immersed themselves in a passionate embrace. Their love advanced, and every touch and every movement was an expression of their deep connection. As they explore each other's bodies, they revel in the power of dynamics that fueled their desire. Franco, known for his strength and confidence, took the lead, his hands guiding Cassandra's body with gentle authority. His touch was firm yet tender as he traced delicate patterns across her skin. His fingers navigated unhurriedly, exploring every curve and crevice, evoking a sense of surrender and trust in Cassandra. It wasn't long before they both climaxed like the great gun of war and lay panting in submission.

Minutes later, Cassandra felt great confidence and, without permission, mounted Franco, and they became locked in a deep penetrating embrace that increased to a steady rhythm that had Franco losing control of the moment and crying out in great ecstasy.

It was not just Franco who revelled in his dominant role. Cassandra, who had always embraced her vulnerability, found immense pleasure in him surrendering control. They relished the knowledge that their submission was a display of strength, not weakness. As

Cassandra's touch intensified, Franco's moan of pleasure filled the room and fulfilled—his desire.

In many other passionate encounters, Franco decided to take the lead. Equally so, Cassandra took on more lead roles than usual. They wanted to show each other their strength and ability to command and fulfill their desires. On encounters, as they kissed passionately, Cassandra's hand explored Franco's body with a newfound confidence. Every touch and caress was an affirmation of their ability to pleasure and dominate. In this profoundly sexual, intimate relationship, the couple forged a connection that transcended societal expectations. They understood that being a man or a woman didn't define their roles; instead, their ability to embrace their desires and explore them together truly mattered.

Throughout the journey, Cassandra and Franco celebrated the fluidity of their desires, challenging the norms that had constrained them for so long. They found joy in breaking down the barriers of what society deems manly or feminine, realizing that true liberation came from embracing their authentic selves. Cassandra and Franco redefined their roles as partners, lovers, and individuals in this modern society. They proved that love, passion, and a deep understanding of each other's desires could create a relationship where traditional gender roles faded into the background. They were a testament to the power of self-discovery, trust, and the beauty of embracing one's desire without prejudice or judgment.

The role of men in sexual intimacy has always shown significant dominance throughout human existence. Sadly, even today, there are still some cultures where men only determine when, how, and frequency of sexual intimacy occurs. With the knowledge that sexual intimacy is a fundamental aspect of human relationships, it contributes holistically to the emotional connection, pleasure, and overall well-being of those who indulge in it.

In the quest for equality and understanding between genders, the traditional roles of men in sexual encounters have undergone considerable transformation in modern society. Men are actively embracing new roles, moving away from outdated stereotypes. They have adapted to the new mindset of equal participation, thus encouraging restored, more engaging, and undoubtedly fulfilling experiences of sexual intimacy. This lesson aims to explore the evolving role of men in sexual encounters and shed light on the importance of shared respect, interaction, and agreement.

Be Done With Stereotypes Already:

The dynamics of dominance in sexual relations have long been a topic of intrigue, study, and debate. Such discussions often revolve around the perceived power imbalances between males and females. When we examine the existence of power dynamics within sexual relationships, it is equally important to approach this conversation with nuance and avoid generalizations. Let us examine the complexities surrounding this phenomenon and seek to acknowledge the complicated nature of this power dynamic that we speak of.

The gender roles and expectations that we see even today are influenced by the manifestation of dominance in sexual relations. Historically, patriarchal structures have assigned men a dominant position in society. This has led to the belief that they should exert control over sexual encounters. However, societal norms are evolving, and the power dynamics within relationships have become more fluid. Many women now embrace their sexual desires and assert their dominance in consensual encounters, which challenges the traditional gender roles.

We have to recognize that individuals possess their unique desires, regardless of their gender roles. Some individuals naturally gravitate towards being the more dominant partner, while others feel more comfortable in assuming the submissive positions, notwithstanding that these preferences are not inherently tied to one gender role over another but rather reflect personal inclinations. It is always vital to avoid assuming that all men desire dominance or that all women prefer submission. These types of assumptions often spread harmful labels, and it takes a lot of work to come away from them.

In this aspect, we must recognize again that the heart of healthy sexual relationships lies within open discussion and approved realms. Dominance, regardless of who embodies it, should always be consensual. Even as we realize that in many intimate settings, roles are mostly assumed and not decided on. Even so, consent allows individuals to establish boundaries and negotiate their power dynamics. This conversation will serve as the foundation on which the relationship rests. It should allow all the parties involved to not just feel safe and respected but also be comfortable in the role that they play in a sexual encounter.

Additionally, it is also important to emphasize that dominance should never involve coercion or the violation of another person's autonomy. Both men and women can derive pleasure from acts of dominance or submission, and these rules can be fluid interchangeably, depending on personal preferences and the consent that's given.

In recent years, discussions surrounding sexual empowerment and liberation have gained real momentum. The movement encourages individuals, irrespective of gender, to embrace their desires, explore their boundaries, and engage in consensual acts that promote mutual pleasure and fulfillment. With that said, we're also seeing greater efforts to bridge this gap.

Rather than viewing male and female dominance in sexual relations as opposing forces, it is more constructive to foster discussion and understanding between the partners with the right understanding and decision. The power dynamics within this relationship warrant two voices in unison in a healthy way. Again, recognizing that the poor dynamics can shift, and change allows for a more equitable exploration of dominance and submission.

Active Participants In Man Talk:

Men are more encouraged to actively engage in open discussions about desired boundaries and consent. This conversation is not necessarily about what they need so much as what their partners also need and require. With regards to men as the focus here, with the right environment that encourages honest and respectful communication, men can help create a space where partners feel comfortable expressing their needs even as they both explore their boundaries. This shift away from mere presumption to a more active dialogue ensures that sexual encounters have a firm basis for understanding and shared pleasure.

Emphasizing Emotional Connection:

In the realm of relationships, emotional connections play an especially important role because they encourage intimacy and strengthen the bond between partners. Historically, though, societal norms have often placed more emphasis on a woman when it comes to emotional expression and connection. However, it is crucial to recognize that men too, have the capacity and the responsibility to cultivate emotional connections with their partners. Men's participation in this process not only enhances their own well-being but also contributes to the overall vigor and longevity of the relationship.

To emphasize emotional connections, men must first recognize that emotions are fundamental to human existence and not only to any specific gender. Therefore, when they acknowledge and embrace their inner fear and attempt to mask emotions, it opens the door for something new and grandeur. Men can also create a safe and supportive space for themselves and their partners to share their innermost feelings. This includes understanding that vulnerability is not a sign of weakness but rather an opportunity for growth and deeper passionate connections.

To emphasize emotional connections, men should actively engage in honest positions with their partners, being aware of both their feelings. Instead of resorting to indifference or avoiding difficult conversations, it is wise to create an environment where they feel comfortable sharing their emotions and actively listening to their partner's experiences. Without actively and realistically listening to their partners, it often leads to misunderstanding and, in extreme cases, separation. When men are not emotionally connected, they are communicating something to their partners, and it is often misread and misunderstood that they are incapable of giving this wonderful thing.

In many cases, it is not necessarily true that the men are not emotionally available. It is more so how they are cultured, and as they grow and learn to express their sexuality, their connectivity with women sometimes challenges them from being the best version of themselves. When the conversations, therefore, open for a better understanding of all the various dynamics happening, you then realize that it was mostly perception, and they have just not been taught how to express their feelings.

Additionally, in most cultures, men are not allowed to become vulnerable, or they are taught to shield their feelings because it shows the depth of being weak and not in control. What usually happens in these cases is that when this behaviour becomes constricted, it is only expressed over a bottle of vodka, at a bar, to other men, who sometimes are not capable of providing the answers or, in some cases, giving the wrong solutions. At the end of the day, the problem usually returns when it is not said, and yet that is the requirement. They, therefore, must learn that empathy, patience, and nonjudgmental attitudes are some key components of effective communication and relationship building. When this is absent, women also withdraw their hearts out of this relationship and seek this emotional connection elsewhere.

Another important factor is the art of active listening. Listening goes beyond just hearing words. It involves utter understanding and empathizing with your own partner. Men should seek to emphasize emotional connection by actively listening to their partner's concerns, desires, and dreams. Most certainly, this requires setting aside distractions and demonstrating genuine interest in their partner's emotional well-being. Active listening does foster trust and encourages vulnerability, yet it straightens emotional bonds between partners.

Men can demonstrate their commitment to emotional connection by providing support and validation to their partners. What is this? This is just offering reassurance, understanding, and encouragement, especially during challenging times. The simple act of acknowledging that their partner's emotions are valid, and their experiences are their frame of reference can create an atmosphere of safety and acceptance. Combined, this acknowledgement fosters emotional intimacy and strengthens their bond even further.

Here, we can examine the simple strategy on how to make this process of emotional connection easier. The boldest step that man can make is to start by looking at shared activities and quality time because that is the foundation on which great relationships are built. When the couple engages in shared activities and spends quality time together, they are putting all the essential ingredients together that build emotional connections. So, by participating in activities that their partner enjoys, men can demonstrate their willingness to invest time and effort into the relationship. Whether it's going on walks, cooking together, or just pursuing mutual hobbies, shared experiences create opportunities for emotional connection and deepen the sense of togetherness.

LESSON EIGHT

Exploring The Limitations Of Sexual Pleasures And Satisfaction In Relationships.

Diane and Roswell lived in a quiet part of London. They were deeply in love, but unlike the traditional norms of society, they had chosen not to marry. They decide that the institution of marriage should not define the strength of their commitment to each other. Diane and Roswell were determined to explore the depth of their relationship, including their intimacy, in a way that transcended societal expectations.

As they embarked on their journey together, Diane and Roswell discovered that external labels did not limit their bond. They understood that genuine connection and fulfillment could be found in the exploration of their desires, both emotional and physical. They sought to understand the intricacies of their bodies and the unique ways in which they could bring pleasure to each other. A fiercely independent woman, Diane had always been curious about her sexuality. She believed true liberation came from embracing her desires without reservation or shame. Roswell, on the other hand, had grown up in a conservative household where sex was considered a taboo topic. However, being with Diane allowed him to break free from those limitations and experience a newfound sense of liberation.

Together, they embark on a mission to discover who they are, exploring their most intimate desires and fantasies. They engage in open and honest conversations, sharing personal experiences that help them understand each other's boundaries and limits. They discovered that sexual pleasure was not confined to physical acts but extended to emotional connection and trust. Diane and Roswell realized that they had the power to redefine their understanding of sexual satisfaction. They learned it wasn't just about the act itself but the intricate and delicate rave of intimacy between their hearts and bodies. They dove into the world of Tantra, discovering ancient practices that allowed them to connect on a deeper level.

Through their exploration, they uncovered the power of touch, the magic of anticipation, and the importance of communication. They learned that vulnerability, trust, and consent were the building blocks of a deeply satisfying sexual relationship. They celebrated each other's pleasure, finding joy in the shared experience of giving and receiving. Their journey was not always easy. They faced moments of insecurity, jealousy, and fear. But they confronted these challenges head-on, understanding that growth came from pushing their boundaries and embracing their vulnerabilities.

As time passed, Diane and Roswell discovered that their relationship exploded beyond the physical. Their exploration of intimacy deepened their emotional connection, allowing them to understand each other's fears, dreams, and aspirations. They realized their bond was a testament to their commitment to one another, irrespective of societal expectations. Diane and Roswell proved that a committed unmarried couple could explore the realms of sexual pleasure and satisfaction beyond the confines of traditional marriage. Their journey taught them that true fulfillment came from embracing only their desires, speaking openly, conversing about what they believed to be satisfying, and nurturing deep emotional connections. Finally, in their exploration, they discovered a genuinely boundless, limitless, and unconditional love.

Without sexual satisfaction, there is no need or desire to engage in this incredible act of sex. Sexual satisfaction is not just a routine but a critical and crucial aspect of any intimate relationship. Overall, its importance transcends all boundaries, serving as a means of bonding, expressing love, and fulfilling physical desires. However, it is essential to acknowledge that every individual sexual preference, desires, and limitations vary. This lesson aims to shed light on the restrictions of sexual pleasures and satisfaction within relationships. It also will attempt to seek restitution by placing emphasis on the need for open interaction, being in one accord, and compromise.

Understanding Different Libidos:

Sex drive is usually called libido. Libido is the term used to describe sexual desire or sex drive. Libido explains the desire for sex outside cultural opinions, biases, or expectations. We learn that hormones, the functioning of the brain, and behaviours, regardless of a person's biological sex, gender identity, or sexual orientation, affect us. Libido can vary from person to person, with some people having what we often refer to as a "high" libido and others having a "low" libido. Libido can also rise and fall due to a person's emotional state, hormone levels, and physical health. Furthermore, there is no numeric measurement for libido or set definition for "normal" libido.

Notwithstanding this fact, a high or low libido is a problem if it messes with relationships, sexual function, or a person's well-being or quality of life. Instead, we understand sex drive in relevant terms. For example, a low libido means a decreased interest or desire in sex. The male libido lives in two areas of the brain: the cerebral cortex and the limbic system. These brain parts are vital to a man's sex drive and performance. They are so important that a man can orgasm simply by thinking or dreaming about a sexual experience.

One of the most common limitations in sexual satisfaction arises from different libidos between partners. Individuals naturally possess varying sexual desires, which can result in relationship imbalances. While one partner may desire frequent intimacy, the other may have a lower libido. This discrepancy can lead to frustration, rejection, and diminished satisfaction. It is crucial for couples to openly discuss their sexual desires and find a compromise that respects both partner's needs.

Physical Limitations:

There are physical limitations that significantly impact sexual satisfaction in intimacy. Chronic illnesses, disabilities, or physical injuries may restrict one's ability to fully engage in specific sexual activities or experience pleasure. It is quite imaginable that if there is chronic arthritis, body aches, and pains, broken limbs, or even some types of skin conditions, intimacy can be affected.

Sex comes with expectations of certain positions, angles, and stimulations. When one partner is not well enough to engage fully in the act, it can cause significant distress in a person and the relationship itself. In such cases, couples must express empathy and identify coordinated approaches to maintain intimacy. This approach is by seeking health care providers or sex therapists, which can be beneficial in finding solutions that accommodate physical limitations.

What Do You Feel For Me?

Sexual satisfaction depends not solely on physical pleasure but emotional connection and intimacy. Whenever any challenges hinder the relationship from living up to its full potential, several feelings will arise. Without a solid emotional bond, the physical act may lack depth and satisfaction. It is no secret that relationship issues can hinder sexual pleasure. Still, couples with unresolved conflicts or emotional disconnection often scarcely recover from the wear and tear and plethora of emotions evoked. Partners need to maintain open lines of communication and emotional support and invest time and effort in nurturing their emotional connection alongside their sexual relationships.

Psychological Factors:

While in one of the previous chapters, we spoke about the psychological factors of sex and sexuality, addressing them in this section of the book is still relevant. Psychological factors such as stress, anxiety, depression, or post-traumas can significantly impact sexual satisfaction. Mental health issues may affect one's libido, ability to experience pleasure, or even engage in sexual activities. It is crucial in this section too, to note that cyclical factors relating to sexually abused people who experienced rape, and degrading circumstances, will affect the pleasures and sexual satisfaction that come with a relationship where intimacy is involved. It is crucial for partners to be understanding, supportive, and encourage seeking professional help if needed. Couples can explore therapy options that address individual and relationship issues to achieve a healthier and more satisfying sexual experience.

Monotony And Routine:

Many couples are not aware that, over time, sexual routines can become quite monotonous and, therefore, lead to decreased satisfaction. Being repetitive in sexual practices and scheduling offers a high probability of boredom that is very likely to dump excitement, novelty, and desires. The recommendation is for couples to make every effort, especially if they place great value on the relationship, to break free from the monotony by exploring new sexual experiences, trying different positions, incorporating role-playing, or even seeking professional advice on spicing up their sexual repertoire. Talking about issues and experimentation can reignite passion and enhance sexual satisfaction within the relationship.

In summary, sexual pleasure and satisfaction in relationships can be influenced by various limitations, including differences in libido, physical constraints, emotional disconnection, psychological factors, and routine. Recognizing and addressing these limitations through clear discussions, empathy, and willingness to compromise can lead to a healthier and more satisfying sexual relationship. By prioritizing emotional connection, exploring alternatives, seeking professional help when needed, and embracing novelty, couples can steer and overcome these limitations to encourage fulfilling and pleasurable sexual bonds.

LESSON NINE

Unveiling The Hidden: How To Identify Red Flags In Intimate Relationships.

Danielle and Stan met at a club in a buzzing neighbourhood in downtown New York. They fell deeply in love and recently got engaged. The entire town was excited as they eagerly planned their upcoming wedding. However, several red flags appeared as the wedding preparations progressed, indicating that Danielle and Stan might not be as compatible as they initially thought.

The first red flag emerged when they started discussing their plans. Danielle had always dreamed of travelling the world and exploring different cultures, while Stan was content with living a simple, quiet life in their hometown. Their differing ideas about the future cost frequent disagreements and clashes, leaving both of them frustrated. The second red flag surfaced during their discussions about finances. Danielle was a meticulous saver, always thinking about the future and making wise financial decisions. On the other hand, Stan was a carefree spender, often indulging in impulsive purchases without considering the consequences. This vast difference in their financial habits created tension and arguments about money.

Furthermore, their communication styles were vastly different. Danielle was a great listener and always tried to express her feelings and concerns openly. However, Stan had a habit of shutting down during conflicts, avoiding discussions, and bottling up his emotions—this lack of effective communication made resolving issues that arose in their relationship increasingly tricky. One more significant red flag was their contrasting social lives. Danielle loved spending time with her friends and family, engaging in social activities, and constantly seeking a new experience. Stan, on the other hand, was more introverted, preferring solitude and quiet nights at home. This difference created a disconnect, as Danielle felt stifled by Stan's need for privacy and lack of interest in socializing.

Despite these red flags wavering in the wind, Danielle and Stan pushed forward with their wedding plans, hoping their love would conquer all. However, as the big day approached, Danielle had a moment of realization. She understood that love alone was insufficient to sustain a healthy, happy relationship. She could not ignore the signs that indicated a fundamental incompatibility between her and Stan. Summoning her courage, Danielle decided to call off the engagement. She knew it would be painful for both of them in the short term, but she believed it was the right choice for their long-term happiness.

Though it was a heart-wrenching experience, Danielle and Stan eventually realized that breaking off the engagement was the best decision for them both. They went their separate ways, allowing themselves the opportunity to find partners who genuinely aligned with their dreams, values, and personalities.

Danielle and Stan learned a valuable lesson: Recognizing and addressing red flags in a relationship is crucial, even if it means making difficult choices. Because, in the end, true compatibility and happiness can only flourish when both individuals are genuinely suited for one another.

Building faith and trust in any intimate relationship can have challenges and insecurities. Intense yearning and accepting that relationships bring joy and companionship and replace inner emptiness makes it more difficult to discern when things are off. However, it is crucial to be aware of potential warning signs, also known as red flags, which may indicate a troubled relationship. Recognizing these indicators as early as dating can help individuals make informed decisions and take necessary steps to protect their emotional well-being. In this lesson, we will explore some common red flags to look out for in intimate relationships.

1. The Lack Of Communication:

Communication is the cornerstone of a healthy relationship; without it, there is no understanding of the direction the relationship is heading. It may be a red flag if you recognize that your partner constantly avoids discussing essential topics, dismisses your concerns, or refuses to engage in open and honest conversations. Lack of communication can lead to misunderstandings, pent-up frustrations, and, finally, a breakdown in trust. When one places great value on a relationship, it should be acknowledged, communicated, and understood. There is more room for speculation by clearly hearing or sharing this fact. Without good communication, there is no assurance of a successful and long-lasting connection.

2. Controlling Behaviors:

Having a controlling partner indicates a lack of independence and insecurity. A controlling partner seeks to exert power and dominance over their significant others. This behaviour is evident in several ways. They may isolate their partner from friends and family, indicate their choices, or constantly monitor their activities. These behaviours are signs of an unhealthy dynamic and can escalate to emotional or physical abuse. Recognizing this red flag and establishing boundaries to protect your autonomy and freedom is essential.

3. Disregards For Boundaries:

Respecting each other's boundaries is crucial in any relationship. Once these boundaries are established and communicated, both parties must mutually accept them. If your partner constantly ignores or violates your physical, emotional, or personal boundaries, it is not a light matter. This behaviour could manifest as pressuring you into unwanted sexual activities, invading your privacy, or dismissing your need for personal space. Having relationships requires mutual respect for boundaries. This red flag is not a simple misunderstanding but be careful not to overlook it and let it go on indefinitely. That is where it will ruin relationships.

4. Constant Criticism:

Constructive criticism is essential to personal growth, but constant belittling and complaints harm a relationship. In some relationships, constant criticism is what some partners endure, and they are oblivious to its meaning and interpretation. Criticism in relationships occurs when a person addresses their concerns in a way that suggests they are finding fault with their partner. These feeling damages relationships because it makes one partner feel as though something about them is bad or wrong. If your partner habitually puts you down, insults you, or undermines your self-esteem, it's a glaring red flag. A healthy partnership should nurture and support each other's growth rather than tearing one another down.

5. Unresolved Anger Or Frequent Explosions:

Anger is a normal human emotion, but when it becomes a frequent event or spirals into forceful or aggressive behaviour, it is a serious red flag. Anger makes people feel more powerful when they cannot express their more vulnerable, underlying emotions. They often precede feelings of frustration, hurt, unmet needs, or perceived injustice. Frequent outbursts of anger, verbal or physical abuse, and threats are signs of deep-seated issues that require addressing. This issue is a serious red flag, and people who wish to save their relationship can seek professional help or consider ending the relationship if such behaviour persists.

6. Dishonesty And Betrayal:

Trust is not just a concept couples must learn about. Instead, it is a subjective experience that must be repeatedly lived and felt. Trust is the foundation of any healthy relationship. With trusting experiences, the relationship offers a secure space for the couple and provides solace and opportunities for deeper sharing and connection. If your partner constantly lies, hides information, or breaks promises, it's a major red flag. This honesty erodes trust, leading to a toxic and unsafe relationship. Restoring trust can be tricky and assessing whether the relationship is worth rescuing is fundamental.

7. Constant Need to Be a Defending Partner

In any relationship, it is common for friends and family members to express concerns about their partners. They may notice behaviours resembling red flags or significant issues that we might overlook and downplay as the individuals involved. The situation can be challenging as it puts us in a position where we must defend our partners while simultaneously questioning whether we are missing something. When faced with such a scenario, it is crucial to approach it with an open mind and consider the perspectives of those around us.

Sometimes, our loved ones can provide valuable insights that we may have been blind to due to our emotional attachment. They may see patterns or behaviours that we are too close to notice, giving them a broader view of the situation. If you experience situations where you constantly defend your partner's credibility or morals to multiple people, there is enough for you to suspect a red flag. Many times, the partner possesses behaviours that are not healthy and raises questions or concerns. Consider this as a red flag. Recognizing red flags in intimate relationships is crucial for maintaining a healthy and fulfilling partnership. By being aware of signs such as lack of communication, controlling behaviour, disregard for boundaries, constant criticism, unresolved anger, and dishonesty, individuals can make informed decisions about the future of their relationships.

Remember, giving precedence to your emotional well-being is critical, and seeking support from friends, family, or professionals can provide valuable guidance during challenging times.

LESSON TEN

Unveiling Deep Penetrating Sexual Desires, Exploring Modern Societies Lust

In the bustling heart of a modern city, a beautiful woman finds herself in the heart of a bisexual enchantment. She unfolds her most authentic identity in a world where sexual taboos and discrimination live. Annalise, a vibrant and confident young woman, exuded an aura of uninhibited sexuality that intrigued those around her.

Annalise would walk into a room with a magnetic presence radiating a glow of confidence and sensuality. Her eyes would fill with mischief, hinting at the world of untamed desires and passions. With each step, her body moves in perfect harmony, drawing attention to her effortless grace. Her appearance reflects her own inhibited sexuality. Her clothing, carefully chosen to accentuate her curves, leaves just enough to the imagination, inviting thoughts of anticipation and allure. Her hair, flowing freely or meticulously styled, framed her face, and added to her aura of raw femininity.

Her words carry a seductive undertone in conversation, laced with innuendos and playfulness. She effortlessly captivates everyone around her and, with charm, leaves them yearning for more. Her laughter is infectious, a combination of joy and a hint of mischief, enticing others to join her in her world of uninhibited pleasure.

The beauty about Annalise is that she embraces her desires without reservation. Unafraid of exploring her passions and indulging in her fantasies, her confidence shines through in every interaction as she fearlessly navigates the intricacies of intimacy and pleasure.

Annalise understands her own body, making no apologies for her wants and needs, and openly communicates them, inviting others to join her in the exploration of their shared desires. Societal norms or expectations do not limit her sexuality. She pushes boundaries and embraces the freedom to express herself fully, unapologetically, embracing her identity and desires. Annalise celebrates her sexuality as a powerful force within her. Yes, it is a source of strength and empowerment.

But beyond her uninhibited sexuality lies a woman of depth and complexity. She possesses a keen intellect, a nurturing spirit, and a compassionate heart. Her sexuality is one facet of her multifaceted being, intertwined with her other qualities to create a captivating and irresistible whole. In her presence, one cannot help but draw to her magnetic energy, intoxicating confidence, and unapologetic embrace of her desires. She's a woman of uninhibited sexuality, a force of nature that leaves an indelible mark on those fortunate to cross her path.

Yet Here We Are: Facing It All:

For centuries, the impact of generations has been by sex and sexuality, the pleasures associated with them, and the world of complexity and intrigue surrounding them. These things are inherent characteristics of human nature, complicatedly laced into the fabric of society. In these modern times, discussions around sexual desires have become more open, allowing for a deeper understanding of the core beliefs and behaviours shaping our sexual landscape.

This lesson will attempt to shed light on the complex aspects of our deep, intimate, penetrating sexual desires and their impact as we exist in this prevailing society.

Why is there interest now? What has prompted this curiosity today? It is simple and yet so profound. It is high time that the information became apparent to those interested in breaking free from oppressive norms. Clarity creates tolerance for individuals to embrace their gender identities.

To understand the core beliefs and behaviours that shape our sexual landscape is also to foster greater empathy, acceptance, and respectful engagement. With continued hope, people embrace stimulating and open dialogue, consent, and ethical exploration. While there are no guarantees, it provides the opportunity for a healthy and fulfilling sexual experience for all individuals.

Sexual Freedom At Last!

Society has witnessed a significant adjustment in sexual beliefs, with an increasing weight on individual freedom and discovery. The assessment of sexual liberation encourages individuals to embrace their desires while adopting a deeper understanding of their needs and preferences. Those days when the words sex, sexuality, and the passions that people feel or even dare to talk about are gone. The concept of liberation has gotten to the level where the question is asked, "Is there even an authority on sexual immorality?"

The last generations have declared significant changes that question even the biblical doctrine and the moral compass that has existed since the beginning. This time in history is unravelling deep sexual desires that allow men and women, women and women, and men and men, the freedom and will even to marry! What a phenomenon! The world has gone mad with sex and what to do with it. No more behind doors, in closets, and behind curtains. Instead, it is on top of the table, on the patio, and in parliament. Wow, is this liberation or what?

Away With Taboos And Stigmas:

Sexual taboos and stigmas grind deep in societies around the world. These taboos can restrict individual expression, create shame, and hinder healthy discussions about sexuality. Sexual desires challenge traditional taboos and the stigma surrounding certain acts or preferences.

Society is gradually becoming more accepting of varied sexual expressions, enabling individuals to explore their desires without fear of judgment or shame. Nonetheless, some people, thankfully, continue to hold on for dear life to their values and refuse to let modern society dictate their behaviour and morally accepted norms. Still, many have happened in these landscapes, where trivial matters center around personal responsibility and choice.

It is time that society started looking at the various strategies to overcome sexual taboos and stigma. Help to reestablish a road map for individuals seeking to navigate and dismantle sexual taboos and stigma. The first step in this regard is to increase education and awareness. In that first step, seek to become educated about the varying changes that are happening in this landscape. It is important to seek reliable information resources such as books, articles, and websites dedicated to sexuality and the whole world of sex. There are also avenues, such as workshops, seminars, or even lectures, which promote healthy discussions around sex and relationships, and more so, the appropriateness or the lack thereof. Educating ourselves can challenge misconceptions and broaden our understanding of diverse sexual orientations, gender identities, and practices.

There is also room to challenge societal norms, as you will further explore in this book. We must recognize that these norms are not fixed or universal but products of culture, history, and power dynamics. Therefore, questioning and challenging these norms actively work towards dismantling them. More than anything else, though, consent and communication play a vital role in all aspects of our sexuality.

Another vital role is that of empathy and understanding. It is crucial to develop compassion and understanding towards others to overcome sexual taboos and stigmas. Recognizing that everyone's sexual journey is unique, it is not our place to judge or shame others based on their choice or experiences. It is a good time to let go of preconceived notions and embrace a mindset of acceptance and support. Overcoming sexual taboos and stigma is an ongoing process that requires personal growth, among other things. Let us, therefore, strive to create a world where everyone can explore their sexuality without fear or shame.

The Communication Platform:

What are people saying about the sexual communication platform being what it is? Good communication is an integral part of all relationships and is essential to any healthy partnership. All relationships do have to deal with difficulties. However, open and straightforward conversations have become the backbone to handle conflict and build a more robust and healthier partnership. Sincere, honest, and effective communication continues to be the key to effectively managing society's woes.

Within the boundaries of sexual intimacy, communication plays a pivotal role in understanding and fulfilling deep sexual desires. The conversations should surround preferences, limitations, and consent cultivated in a safe environment. It also encompasses the exploring and satisfying components of these desires within the context of consensual relationships.

There are factors such as to marry or to live in celibacy, heterosexual interaction versus homosexuality, and the list goes on. These factors should be center stage, even as one attempts to understand how to communicate matters of intimacy without being judged or influenced. However, in a broader spectrum, greater awareness exists with more platforms to express needs, perspectives, and aspirations.

The Influence Of Media And Technology:

One must admit though, that today's media is more vocal than ever. Modern media and technology have indisputably shaped and exaggerated sexual desires. The prevalence of explicit content and online platforms has accelerated the exposure to various sexual experiences, fantasies, and fetishes. While this can be empowering, it raises concerns about unrealistic expectations and potential addiction. The primary advertising of food and juices reflects sexism and major lust, even pervasive, in the face of children and teens. Society is not sufficiently creating culturally accepted persuasions, but what to do?

The Psychological Aspect:

Psychology is the study of human emotions, behaviours, and actions. A reflection in history confirms that psychology played a pivotal role as we explore perspectives on sexual desires. Their origins and their impact on our progression influence and shape how we exist and operate. In the context of our profoundly probing sexual desires, they often stem from complicated psychological factors. A better understanding of the psychological foundations of these desires, such as past experiences, fantasies, or emotional needs, can contribute to a more excellent grasp of self and the motivation behind deep-seated desires.

The Freudian View:

Sigmund Freud, a prominent figure in the field of psychology, transformed our understanding of the human mind and behaviour. Among his theories, Freud is famously known for his beliefs on sexual desires and their role in shaping human behaviour. Freud maintained that sexual desires and instincts were fundamental characteristics of human nature. He proposed the concept of libido, which refers to the energy associated with sexual drives.

According to Freud, libido is crucial in driving human behaviour and determining psychological development. One of Freud's most significant theories concerning sexual desires is the Oedipus Complex. He argued that during childhood, individuals experience unconscious sexual desires toward their opposite-sex parents while experiencing jealousy and rivalry between their same-sex parents. The Oedipus complex got its name from the Greek mythological character Oedipus. Freud believed this phenomenon occurs at a crucial developmental stage, the Phallic stage, between the ages of three and five.

Freud also theorized that there is a vital role of the unconscious mind in shaping sexual desires. He postulated that sexual desires and fantasies get repressed due to societal norms and moral restrictions. These repressed desires, he felt, then resided in the unconscious mind, manipulating your influencing thoughts, feelings, and behaviours.

Freud argued that understanding and addressing these unconscious sexual desires were essential for psychological well-being. Furthermore, he proposed various psychosexual stages of development, each characterized by different erogenous zones and associated sexual desires. The developmental stages he named: the oral, anal, phallic, latency, and genital stages, each with developmental timelines.

Critics argued that Freud's theory on sexual desires was overly focused on the significance of sexual factors and often lacked empirical evidence. Despite these criticisms, his ideas continue to influence the field of psychology and have shaped our understanding of human sexuality. Some of these underpinnings are evident in human nature in the present day. One must look objectively and watch as the parents and society seek to groom our children and youth. As they navigate life, this observation will prove the sexual developmental stages that echo Freudian sentiments.

The Role Of Consent And Ethical Exploration:

In the quest to find fulfilling sexual desires, it is vital to emphasize the critical role of consent and ethics as willing participants. The use of consent protects all parties involved, which means forced sex, rape, and all the other sexual atrocities are not okay, and a person's rights and choices will have a firm footing in lawful circumstances. It goes as far as to dictate to husbands their wives have the option to say, "Not tonight," and it holds meaning. Ethics dictates that boundaries and limits create honour and respect. This way, harm or exploitation is limited to everyone, including vulnerable populations. Even with the best of law, the lust for sex and all its tenets permeates harm that scares many innocents.

LESSON ELEVEN

Embracing Sexual Diversity, Paving The Way For A More Inclusive Society

Harmony Ville is a community that constantly evolves with a youthful generation who actively participate in community-based activities, which has been an example to neighbouring communities. In this community, a group of individuals came together to embrace sexual diversity and pave the way for a more inclusive society. They believed in celebrating love in all of its forms and wanted to create a safe space where everyone could express their true selves without fear of judgment or discrimination.

In the heart of the city, they established a community center called "Unity House." The building buzzed with excitement as people from all levels of society gathered to share their stories, experiences, and knowledge. The center offered workshops, support groups, and educational programs to promote understanding and acceptance.

One sunny afternoon, a young woman named Monica walked into Unity House, feeling uncertain and anxious. Monica had recently come to terms with her bisexuality but was troubled to find acceptance within her family and social circle. As she stepped inside, Deon greeted her, a warm-hearted volunteer who had faced similar challenges in their journey as a transgender person. Deon listened intently to Monica's worries and shared their experience of overcoming prejudice, offering encouragement and support.

Inspired by Deon's kindness, Monica joined a support group for LGBTQ+ youth at Unity House. There, she met others who had faced similar struggles and found solace in sharing their stories. Together, they organized events and campaigns to raise awareness about sexual diversity, aiming to dispel stereotypes and foster expectations within the community.

One evening, Unity House hosted a panel discussion on LGBTQ+ rights, inviting community leaders, activists, and allies to participate. The panelists shared personal anecdotes and highlighted the importance of inclusivity and equal rights. The event empowered attendees to challenge their own biases and engage in open dialogue, ultimately fostering a deeper understanding of their sexual diversity.

As words spread about Unity House and its impactful work, more individuals from the city began to embrace and celebrate sexual diversity. Neighbours who had been hesitant or uninformed found themselves attending workshops on gender identity and sexual orientation, eager to learn and grow. Gradually, acceptance and respect became the norm rather than the exception in Harmony Ville.

Emboldened by the positive changes they had witnessed, the community members of Unity House decided to organize a pride parade in the heart of the city. With colourful flags waving high and music filling the streets, people of all ages came together to celebrate love and acceptance. Families, friends, and even local businesses showed their commitment to creating a more inclusive society. The pride parade became an annual tradition, growing each year, and Harmony Ville soon became known as a beacon of acceptance and respect for sexual diversity. Unity House continues to thrive, providing a haven for those in need and supporting individuals on their journey of self-discovery.

Through their dedication and unwavering belief in the power of love, the community members of Harmony Ville proved that embracing sexual diversity could pave the way for a more inclusive society. They showed that we can create a world where everyone can live and love freely by standing united, celebrating differences, and treating one another with compassion.

In today's modern society, sexual diversity is no longer a topic whispered behind closed doors. It has emerged as a powerful force, shaping our understanding of human sexuality and challenging traditional norms. Sexual orientation once considered a private matter, is now recognized as a significant aspect of personal identity, playing a contributory role in the richness and range of our collective human experience. This lesson explores how sexual diversity impacts society, fostering acceptance, inclusion, and celebrating individuality in this new era.

The Spectrum Of Sexual Orientation:

The vast spectrum of sexual orientation involves several perspectives, including heterosexuality, homosexuality, bisexuality, pansexuality, asexuality, and more. Each orientation represents a unique way individuals experience attraction and form intimate connections. This expanding understanding of sexual orientation acknowledges that love and attraction can transcend gender, allowing individuals to express their authentic selves without fear of judgment or discrimination. While this may be so, some levels of society are not yet ready to tolerate, get on board with, or acknowledge the varying viewpoints. Certain echelons of society blatantly refuse to engage in the discussion about there even being a choice.

The Breaking Down Of Stereotypes:

The recognition and acceptance of sexual diversity have profoundly impacted society. It has opened an avenue for dialogue, education, and understanding to foster a more inclusive and empathetic community. Individuals can create change by challenging outdated prejudices and creating space for individuals to explore their identities. The hope is that openness and change will improve mental health, self-acceptance, and overall well-being.

The whole sphere of sexual diversity has dismantled harmful stereotypes that have plagued society for so long. It forces us to view individuals based on their character, talents, and contributions rather than their sexual orientation. As these lifestyle changes occur in this new era, the stigma surrounding LGBTQ-plus individuals dissolves, allowing them to live authentically and contribute fully to all aspects of life, from educational careers to family and relationships.

The Promotion Of Equality And Rights:

Recognizing sexual diversity has paved the way for significant advancements in equal rights. Many countries have adopted legislation to protect LGBTQ-plus individuals from discrimination, ensuring their access to employment, housing, healthcare, and education. These legal and societal changes mark crucial steps toward dismantling systemic and religious barriers and achieving true equality.

Enriching Intersectionality:

Recognizing and understanding that individuals have multiple identities that intersect and influence their experience is essential. We must also remember that people face discrimination or marginalization due to their sexual orientation, gender identity, race, ethnicity, religion, disability, socioeconomic status, etc. All these factors are connected in some ways and, therefore, will affect people's lives in various ways.

While these multiplicities of issues may never affect a large percentage of the population, those who get blessings as non-victims, along with more vital voices, will have to endeavour to create a safe space to validate the feelings of others. By creating safe and nonjudgmental spaces, we cater to the affected so that they can share their experiences; we will thus learn to listen attentively without interrupting or dismissing their feelings. We must also attempt to validate their emotions, affirm their identities, and accept that their perspectives are valid and valuable.

It is not always easy to embrace intersectionality, so an essential aspect of supporting this phenomenon is examining and challenging your biases. It is wise to solely reflect on our own beliefs and prejudices and actively work towards dismantling them. In this regard, the art of self-reflection is mainly tested and confronted. However, seeking feedback from others and being open to learning and growing can make this process easier. This process also includes reading books, articles, and research papers written by diverse authors that explore different aspects of this phenomenon.

We also must pay attention to the amplified diverse voices. These are the voices where we share experiences and perspectives, where people pay attention to their stories and struggles and triumphs. Varying voices can be amplified by sharing their work, promoting their platforms, and engaging in meaningful dialogue.

Advocacy and support are another opportunity to embrace intersectionality. Speaking up against discrimination, prejudice, and stereotypes is high time. Instead, we must use our privilege to advocate for equal rights and justice, including fair treatment for everyone. The support organizations can do well with the support to promote initiatives and policies that encourage inclusivity and protect the rights of diverse populations.

As we support the diverse population as defined in intersectionality, we, in turn, support mental health. Many people in these target groups experience significant mental health issues, which could be why they diversify in the first place. Be willing to provide counselling services or support groups to help individuals navigate their challenges. Remember, enriching intersectionality is an ongoing process that requires continuous learning, self-reflection, and active engagement. It creates a more inclusive and equitable world for all individuals, irrespective of their intersecting identities.

Sexual diversity intersects with other aspects of identity, such as race, ethnicity, religion, and ability. Being aware of these intersections proves vital as we endeavour to understand individuals' unique and varied life situations. We are promoting an inclusive society that embraces diversity in all its forms. Recognizing and celebrating the complex tapestry of identities creates a more vibrant and enriching world for everyone.

Regardless of how we view sexual diversity, it has emerged as a transformative force in this era, giving rise to things we once saw as norms, challenging those norms while fostering acceptance. By embracing sexual orientation as an integral part of personal identity, we promote inclusivity, equality, and the celebration of individuality. As we strive for a more inclusive society, let us cherish and uplift the diversity within our communities, recognizing that love knows no boundaries and that everyone deserves respect and acceptance, regardless of their sexual orientation.

LESSON TWELVE

The Evolving Narrative Of Sex And Its Position In Today's Modern Society

In the busy city of Metropolis, a diverse group of individuals lived. Their lives intertwined to demonstrate the evolving narrative of sex and its position in today's modern society. Everyone has a unique story, shedding light on meaningful discussions and challenging societal norms. First, there was Jada, a passionate advocate for sexual liberation and gender equality. Jada worked tirelessly at a local nonprofit, organizing workshops and events to educate people about consent, healthy relationships, and the importance of open communication. She believed sex should be a consensual and essential experience for everyone involved.

Next was Randall, an art collector who challenged traditional gender norms through artwork. Randall's thought-provoking pieces explored the fluidity of sexual identity and the beauty of self-expression. His work sparked conversations and encouraged others to question the binary understanding of sex and gender.

In the same community, we find Nerissa, a middle-aged woman who had recently come out as a lesbian after years of suppressing her true identity. Nerissa's journey of self-discovery demonstrated the importance of acceptance and the freedom of embracing one's sexuality. Her story resonated with many who had struggled with societal expectations and internalized homophobia.

Meanwhile, Marvin, a middle-aged man, confronted the stigma surrounding male sexuality and mental health. Marvin openly shared his experiences with erectile dysfunction and sought therapy to address the underlying psychological factors. His vulnerability and willingness to seek help challenged the notion that men should always conform to societal expectations, opening up conversations about men's sexual health.

In the heart of Metropolis, there was a thriving LGBTQ+ Community Center where individuals like Randall, Marvin, Nerissa, and Jada found solace and support. The center provided a safe space for people to explore their identities, engage in meaningful discussions, and access resources related to sexual health and relationships.

One day, the Community Center organized a panel discussion on comprehensive sex education in schools. Jada, Randall, Marvin, and Nerissa got an invitation to share their experiences and perspectives. The panel sparked a spirited debate about the importance of inclusive sex education that covered topics such as consent, sexual orientation, and gender identity. Parents, educators, and policymakers attended the event, and the discussion initiated a dialogue that would eventually lead to positive changes in the local education system.

Through their stories and experiences, Jada, Nerissa, Randall, and Marvin exemplified the evolving narrative of sex in today's modern society. They challenged stereotypes, fought for inclusivity, and advocated for open conversations about sex and sexuality. Their collective efforts contributed to a more accepting and understanding community where people felt empowered to embrace their authentic selves and engage in healthy, consensual relationships.

Together, they demonstrated that sex is a multifaceted aspect of human life, deserving respect, understanding, and ongoing conversation. By sharing their narratives, they inspired others to challenge societal norms, dismantle prejudices, and create a more inclusive and sex-positive world.

While sex continues to dominate parts of human nature and plays a significant role in human development, the perception and understanding of sex have endured an extensive transformation. This lesson investigates the evolving narrative surrounding sex and its position in contemporary society. We will seek to explore the factors contributing to these changes and the implications they carry.

The Status Of Taboos And Stigma:

One of the most noticeable shifts in society's perception of sex is the breaking down of traditional taboos and the long-held stigmas. Our communities have transformed into a more liberal and open-minded culture. Discussions around sexuality, sexual orientation, and gender identity have become more prevalent. This increased awareness and acceptance have led to a more inclusive and diverse understanding of sex, giving individuals the freedom to express themselves authentically. Notably, gay relationships have become more prevalent in some societies. Sexual styles and acceptable boundaries are a big thing—things such as anal or oral sex. They seem to have exploded cultural barriers and are dominating the landscape of sexual desires.

Gay marriage is being accepted and recognized in the upper echelons of modern societies and some states and provinces. Many believe the church has lowered its voice and is cowered, even with freedom of expression. Still, people can freely express their opinions and practice intimate phrases without fear and abuse.

Empowering Sexual Education:

Modern society recognizes the importance of comprehensive sexual education. Schools and other institutions are prioritizing teaching about consent, safe sex practices, and the importance of healthy relationships. By providing individuals with greater awareness and understanding, society aims to promote responsible sexual behaviour, reduce the spread of sexually transmitted infections, and empower individuals to make informed choices about their bodies.

Some educational institutions have now embraced a curriculum that teaches the younger generation about sex and sexual orientation. Partially, the design of these curricula enables people to choose who they want to identify as in the world of sexual beings. It has gotten to the level where parents no longer decide what sex their children are. Children can now, within the education system, decide if they want to present themselves as males or females, regardless of the biological evidence that presents itself.

Embracing Sexual Liberation:

Sexual liberation is the freedom to explore and express sexuality without judgment or societal constraints. Society increasingly acknowledges that consensual sexual experiences can be healthy and beneficial for individuals. This shift signifies the departure from the previous notion that sex should be confined to procreation or within the boundaries of a traditional monogamous relationship.

Access to contraception, abortion, and divorce are now more than ever. Sexual relations are no longer mandatory as part of marriage, and sexual life and procreation outside marriage are no longer stigmatized and asserted in some instances. People embrace their desires and preferences and explore alternative relationship structures such as consensual non-monogamy.

Technology And The Digital Age:

Through the rapid progression of technology and the rise of the digital age, the landscape of sex and relationships is noticeably impacted. Technology has given rise to online dating apps, virtual intimacy, and long-distance relationships. These trends have normalized, allowing individuals to connect and explore their sexuality beyond physical boundaries. Still, with the glamour and glitter, this digital landscape also presents challenges, giving rise to privacy concerns, cyber harassment concerns, and the act of being objective to individuals. Society must navigate these complexities in this new age and establish ethical parameters to ensure a safe and respectful online environment.

Addressing Societal Issues:

Sexual freedom and the changing dynamics of relationships have also brought to light various societal issues that demand attention. These include consent violations, sexual harassment, and gender inequality. In cultures where so much seems to be around intimacy and lust combined, society can work towards creating safer spaces, fostering gender equality, and promoting a culture of respect, consent, and accountability. By talking about the varying issues and openly resolving them, it is the best way.

LESSON THIRTEEN

Sexual Perspective To Navigate Intimacy In Today's Modern Society

In this modern society, there are varying perspectives on navigating intimacy, and it continues to challenge the views and experiences of individuals like never before. Amidst the shifting landscape, a man grapples with the complexities and nuances arising from this intimate conversation.

Meet Ethan, an assertive thirty-one-year-old professional navigating the intricate web of relationships, desires, and societal expectations. Unlike previous generations, he finds himself in a world where open conversations about sex are becoming more common, and traditional notions of intimacy are now redefined. A man who once revelled in intimacy with older, more mature women suddenly falls prey to older, more mature men.

Being open-minded and reflective, Ethan recognizes the importance of consent, communication, and respect in all sexual encounters. He understands sex is a shared experience and prioritizes enthusiastic and affirmative consent, ensuring both parties feel comfortable and empowered. In this evolving narrative of sex, Ethan has embraced the concept of sexual fluidity, acknowledging that human sexuality is a spectrum. While he respects and supports individuals who identify across the spectrum, he understands that sexual orientation and gender identity are unique to each person's journey. So, as he journeys through this life, he also embraces who he is.

Ethan also recognizes the influence of technology in this modern sexual age. He gets on online dating apps and is so engrossed in this revolutionized era of how people connect. Online dating apps also enable him to explore his desires and preferences with a broader pool of potential partners. However, he also acknowledges that they need caution and discretion in this digital realm, understanding the importance of online safety and consent.

As he embraces the evolving narrative of sex, Ethan also encounters challenges. He grapples with the pressure to conform to societal expectations, questioning the stereotypes and gender roles that persist in the modern age. He seeks to break free from the constraints imposed by society, embracing his desires and exploring his boundaries.

Through it all, Ethan strived to maintain a healthy and balanced approach to his sex life. He understands the importance of sexual education for himself and others, promoting open dialogue and destigmatizing conversations around sexual health and pleasure.

Living in this modern society with the evolving narrative of sex, Ethan is a man who seeks to navigate the complexities with empathy, respect, and understanding. He embraces changes, challenges the norms, and strives to create a more inclusive and accepting environment for all partners to express their sexuality freely and authentically.

The Cultural And Gender Equality Perspectives:

Sexual attitudes, behaviours, and practices vary significantly across cultures, reflecting deep-rooted beliefs, values, and traditions. In some societies, sex may be regarded as taboo, while in others, it is openly discussed and celebrated. Recognizing and respecting different cultural perspectives on sex allows us to embrace diversity and challenge ethnocentric prejudices.

As we examine sex through a gender lens, we must address the whole power dynamics. Historically, in promoting equality, societal norms often dictate that men should be assertive and sexually dominant while women should be passive and submissive. Today, society will not have any such thing, and the practice is less prevalent in certain classes within this same society. Presently, there is less bias as people strive for gender equality, acknowledging that both men and women have the right to express their desires and boundaries, free from societal pressures and stereotypes.

Exploring LGBTQ+ - Who They Are:

Historically, societies have had varied attitudes towards sex and sexuality, especially in the Lesbians, Gays, Bisexual, Transgender, Queer and Others (LGBTQ+) communities. Many ancient civilizations celebrated and embraced diverse sexual practices and expressions. In fact, Ancient Greece is known for its approval of same-sex relationships and the flexibility of sexual identities. In contrast, other civilizations have imposed strict moral and religious codes that regulate sexual behaviours while suppressing specific sexual orientations. These restrictions often cause great stigmatizing and marginalizing of those who deviate from societal norms.

Recognizing the experiences and perspectives of the LGBTQ+ community is crucial in understanding sex in modern society. Sexual orientation and gender identity are diverse, and part of society believes that everyone deserves respect, acceptance, and equal rights. The argument is that creating an inclusive environment fosters a community where individuals can explore and express their sexuality authentically, without fear or discrimination.

The Conversation Around Permission:

The importance of consent cannot be overstated in today's discussions about sex. The conversation around permission must come from a place of passion, should be ongoing, and freely given by all parties with respect to intimacy. The encouragement of open, frank conversations about sexual desires, personal boundaries, and romantic expectations creates a foundation of respect and mutual understanding. With regards to all sexual matters or concerns, by prioritizing permission to explore options as part of the ongoing discussion, the act of promoting healthy sexual relationships that are built on trust, safety, and consent will be normalized.

The Inclusion Of Education And Empowerment:

A comprehensive and inclusive sex education approach is fundamental today. Educating individuals about the diverse perspectives, experiences, and practices surrounding sex helps dispel myths and misconceptions. Such a sex education approach should seek to reduce stigma, break down invisible barriers, and allow for greater understanding. Empowering individuals with knowledgeable consent, safe sex practices, and emotional intimacy aspects equips them to make informed decisions and promote their overall well-being.

This lesson, therefore, summarizes that sexuality is a deep, personal, and nuanced aspect of human life, shaped by the various perspectives in modern society. By recognizing and embracing diverse perspectives on sex, culture, gender-based, or LGBTQ+, we can create a more inclusive, empathetic, and respectful culture.

Enhancement, navigating the educational platforms, and a commitment to upholding the principles of consent, communication, and equality will give rise to inclusion. By doing so, we can symbolically embrace while promoting healthy relationships, celebrate the visuality, and promote sexual well-being for all.

LESSON FOURTEEN

Embracing Sexuality And Singlehood: Navigating Relationships In The Modern Age

Years ago, in the bustling city of Hammondville lived a sweet and affectionate woman known as Maya. Maya had experienced her fair share of heartbreaks and disappointments in the realm of love. After years of failed relationships, she decided to embark on a journey of self-discovery and embrace the beauty of living a fulfilling single life. Maya had low self-esteem and allowed her past partners to define who she was. Maya lost herself in the person she became, and each time those relationships ended, she redefined again in new ones.

When the last relationship ended quite abruptly without explaining what really happened, Maya's mind reeled in grave confusion, and she almost lost her mind. Maya travailed many heartbreaks that left her feeling used, brutalized, feeling like a failure, and, more times than once, no desire to continue living. Months passed, and all she could see was bleak and an emotionally frail single woman, reflecting from her full-length mirror in a corner of her tiny apartment. After much prodding and support from friends and her church family, Maya finally decided to embrace her sexuality, recognizing that her desires and passions were essential to her identity. She deserved more, as this was the avenue for healing.

Two years slipped by, and as the months passed slowly, so did her insecurities, loneliness, and self-hate. Before long, however, a confident woman emerged who knew how to find joy in her own company. She revelled in the freedom of being single and unburdened by the expectations and compromises often accompanying romantic relationships. Maya indulged in her love for dance, joining a local dance studio where she would express herself through movement. Her body became her canvas, and she painted it with sensual grace, captivating the audience every time she performed. Through her dance, she conveyed a powerful message of self-love and sensuality, inspiring others to embrace their lifestyle and desires.

Maya also thrived in her professional life. As an architect, she poured her creativity into designing magnificent structures, which was a testament to her talent. Maya's work reflected her fears, independence, and unwavering determination regardless of her not-so-long, very disturbing past. She revealed the satisfaction of bringing her visions to life, leaving a lasting mark on her loved city.

In her free time, Maya explored her passions and interests. She delved into literature, losing herself in enchanting worlds created by talented authors. She studied books on philosophy, psychology, and sexuality, expanding her knowledge and understanding of herself and others. Maya attended workshops and seminars, engaging in thought-provoking discussions that further enriched her life.

Maya's friendships were an integral part of her fulfilling life. She surrounded herself with diverse individuals who shared her zest for life and celebrated her independence. They delighted in deep conversations filled with laughter, support, and understanding. Maya's friends admired her for her strength and welcomed her sexuality without judgment or prejudice. While Maya accepted her sexuality alone, she did not shy away from exploring her desires with like-minded individuals. She enjoyed the thrill of casual encounters, understanding that physical intimacy could express self-love and exploration. Maya had learned to differentiate between love and lust, knowing that her sexuality was a powerful force that required celebration without needing a committed relationship.

Maya's journey of self-discovery led her to a profound realization as time passed. She learned that fulfillment didn't solely rely on romantic love but was a culmination of self-acceptance, personal growth, and embracing her desires. Maya's decision to live single testified to her strength, resilience, and unwavering belief that she was enough, just as she was. In a world that often equated happiness with finding "the one." Maya's story shattered stereotypes and societal expectations. She proved that one could lead a fulfilling life, embracing her sexuality and independence without relying on someone else for validation. Maya became an inspiration for many, a symbol of empowerment and self-love. Maya continued to waltz through life, unapologetically embracing her sexuality and living her own life.

The Unraveling:

In today's fast-paced world, the dynamics of relationships and sexuality have undergone tremendous transformations. Being single no longer carries the stigma it once did, allowing individuals to embrace their sexuality and explore diverse avenues of personal enrichment. This lesson, therefore, aims to shed light on the evolving landscape of living single as a sexual being. It highlights the prospects and challenges of pursuing a fulfilling and empowered life.

Exploring Sexual Liberation:

The modern age has observed an immense shift towards sexual liberation. People are more open about their desires, preferences, and identities. This shift has created a supportive environment for singles to explore their sexuality without judgment. This newfound freedom encourages individuals to engage in more viable conversations, experiment with different experiences, and build a strong foundation of self-awareness and acceptance.

Embracing Personal Growth:

Being single provides an exclusive prospect for personal growth and self-discovery. Without the constraints of a committed relationship, individuals can focus on themselves, nurture their passions, and develop a strong sense of identity. This period of self-exploration allows people to understand their desires and boundaries.

An essential aspect of this self-discovery pursuit is that it aids individuals in exploring choices regarding sexual encounters or potential relationships. Regardless of how one may feel about living single, it is the opportune time to cultivate greater awareness and connect with self on a deeper level. During these times, personal goals are created and explored.

Social media has glamourized intimate relationships, and this false presentation of security and success misleads many. Looking from the perspective where more evidence points to happiness being without an intimate partnership, now is a perfectly reasonable time to use your singlehood to get personal goals and work towards achieving them. While single, adopting beneficial relationships with friends, family, and community is also essential. Surround oneself with supportive individuals who uplift and inspire. Engage in meaningful conversations, participate in social activities, and contribute to causes that resonate and create satisfaction. After all, building solid connections and investing in relationships will formulate a sense of belonging and support essential for growth.

Gaining education about different aspects of sexuality, such as harmony, interaction, and pleasure, offers an exhilarating sensation. An important part of that is to consider experimenting with self-pleasure and self-discovery for a deeper understanding of your own body and desires. The journey of self-exploration can lead to increased confidence, self-acceptance, and a healthier attitude towards intimacy.

Navigating Casual Relationships:

Nowadays, casual relationships have become more rampant, and many singles choose to engage in consensual, non-committed encounters. Such relationships can empower people to explore their desires while maintaining emotional autonomy. However, it is crucial to establish clear boundaries and ensure that both parties are on the same page. Otherwise, potential misunderstandings or hurt feelings can be very unforgiving. There lies the risk of trauma associations without appropriate measures, leading to lawful proceedings and therapy requirements.

The Rise Of Online Dating For Singles:

The introduction of dating apps and online platforms has transformed how singles connect and explore their sexual and romantic interests. These platforms provide a convenient and accessible path to meet like-minded individuals, forging connections that may not have been possible otherwise. Nonetheless, it is essential to approach online dating with caution. This modern phenomenon has its dangers, especially as it can bring challenges such as ghosting, catfishing, or shallow interactions.

Ghosting is a term used to describe abruptly or intentionally cutting off all communication with someone. Ghosting usually occurs in a personal or romantic relationship without any explanation or warning. It typically occurs when one person seizes to respond to calls, texts, or any other communication, effectively disappearing from another person's life.

This term has gained popularity in modern dating, becoming increasingly familiar with the rise of online dating platforms and digital communication. Ghosting can leave the person with the experience feeling confused, hurt, and rejected. It is complicated when the person has lived without closure or understanding of what went wrong.

On the other hand, catfishing refers to creating a fake online persona or identity, usually on social media or dating sites. They design this persona primarily to deceive someone, which can be traumatic at the end of the day. The person who engages in catfishing pretends to be someone they are not, and they often use fake photos, names, and personal information to establish this false identity. Many people create catfishing on this online platform for various reasons, such as seeking attention, emotional manipulation, financial scams, or even as a form of cyberbullying. Several people become victims of catfishing when they are tricked into forming an emotional connection or relationship with a false identity, unaware of the deception.

These two concepts of ghosting and catfishing can have significant emotional and psychological effects on the individuals involved. When there are also insecurities, ghosting can compound the situation and lead to feelings of rejection, self-doubt, and a loss of trust in future relationships. The same catfishing can result in emotional trauma and damage one's self-esteem, leaving victims feeling deceived, betrayed, and violated.

Therefore, It is essential to approach online interactions with caution, ensuring authenticity and maintaining open communication to prevent these harmful behaviours. Maintaining open communication, setting realistic expectations, and prioritizing personal safety, are vital when navigating online dating. It is encouraged to become more perceptive in this unfolding yet exciting sphere of online dating.

The Self-Empowered And Emotional Me:

What exactly is the essence of this lesson? Being single allows individuals to prioritize their emotional well-being and focus on self-empowerment. By cultivating a staunch support system, engaging in self-care practices, and pursuing personal goals, singles can find fulfillment beyond romantic or sexual relationships. Recognizing that self-love and self-worth are not contingent on being in a partnership enables individuals to embrace their single status with confidence and commitment.

In the modern age, being single and embracing one's sexuality is no longer seen as a limitation but as an opportunity for personal growth, self-exploration, and empowerment. The evolving landscape of relationships encourages individuals to navigate casual encounters, explore online dating platforms, and prioritize emotional well-being. By embracing the freedom of being single, individuals can build a fulfilling life that celebrates their individuality, desires, and aspirations.

LESSON FIFTEEN

Embracing Solitude, Navigating The Modern Age Of Sexual Cravings As A Single Individual

In the bustling city of New York, a young man called Jared lived. He was an ordinary man with extraordinary determination. Jared always surrounded himself with people, drawn to the city's energy. However, as he grew older, he craved something different: solitude. Jared had witnessed the destructive powers of unhealthy relationships and behaviour in his friends' lives. He saw how the pursuit of fleeting pleasure often left them feeling empty and unfulfilled. Determined not to repeat their mistakes, Jared consciously navigated the modern age of sexual cravings with outstanding commitment.

He started by reevaluating his priorities. Jared realized that true happiness and fulfillment could only come from within. Like most other characters in this intriguing book, he also embarked on a journey of self-discovery, embracing solitude as an opportunity for personal development. Instead of seeking validation from others, he sought assurance from himself. In a world where instant gratification had become the norm, Jared resisted indulging in superficial relationships. He focused on building deeper connections with his friends and family, nurturing genuine bonds that stood the test of time. He found solace in their company, cherishing every moment spent together.

Jared also recognized the importance of self-care. He dedicated himself to physical fitness, not to attract others but as a way to maintain a healthy lifestyle and feel good about himself. Jared sought solace in nature, often venturing into the city's parks and immersing himself in the beauty of the world around him. It was during these moments that he truly felt connected to himself.

This modern age bombarded Jared with temptations at every turn. Yet, he remained steadfast in his commitment to resisting unhealthy behaviours. He redirected his energy towards cultivating his passions and pursuing meaningful hobbies. He threw himself into his work, excelled in his career, and found purpose in his accomplishments.

As time passed, Jared realized that embracing solitude had not isolated him; it had set him free. He discovered an inner peace that he had never experienced before. The cravings for validation and unhealthy relationships gradually faded, replaced by a deep sense of contentment and self-assurance. Jared's commitment to his journey of self-discovery inspired those around him. Friends began to seek his advice, drawn to his unwavering resolve in the face of temptation. He became a beacon of hope in a world consumed by instant gratification.

In the end, Jared's commitment to embracing solitude and resisting the allure of unhealthy relationships and behaviours brought him a sense of fulfillment that surpassed anything he had ever imagined. His definition of who he was, was no longer by his cravings but by his unwavering dedication to personal growth and self-love.

As Jared continued to navigate the modern age, he did so with outstanding commitment, embracing solitude to find his true self. In doing so, he discovered that the most valuable relationship he could ever have was the one he had with himself.

Solitude in a sexually stimulating modern age can pose unique challenges for single people. With societal norms often elaborating on the trilling dynamics of romantic relationships and the endless revelation of sexual imagery, it can be easy to feel lonely or pressured to find a partner. However, being single in this era also represents countless opportunities for personal growth, self-discovery, and the freedom to navigate everyone's journey. Let us delve into the complexities faced by single individuals in a sexually craved modern age as we explore how to embrace solitude with confidence.

Finding Relationships:

Admittedly, we are part of a society that prioritizes physical intimacy. It is essential to redefine the meaning of relationships. Sometimes, our lives are consumed with overwhelming divisions, even though many areas do not bring significant fulfillment. Being single allows individuals to explore all types of human connections, such as deep friendships, mentorships, or even a stronger bond with oneself. The recommendation, therefore, is to broaden our understanding of relationships so we can embrace the richness of human connections beyond romantic or sexual involvement. Take advantage of this solitude to invest time in self-care, self-reflection, and self-improvement. Engaging in activities that bring joy, learning new skills, and nurturing passions can help develop a strong self of self-worth, making one less reliant on external validation.

Challenging Societal Pressures:

Amidst all the other occurrences in this new era, it is necessary to challenge societal pressures that suggest being single is undesirable or incomplete. Indeed, everyone should be aware that one's happiness and fulfillment do not solely depend on being in a romantic relationship. Instead, it is a new opportunity to grip the freedom to make choices without compromising personal values or desires. By reframing societal norms, single individuals do not just focus on personal growth but also create fulfilling lives on their terms.

Navigating Sexual Cravings:

The constant exposure to pornography and uncanny intimate occurrences can prove compelling for single individuals in this sexually craved modern age. People often compromise without a healthy and responsible manner to address these cravings. A first step to dealing with these internal realities is to acknowledge that the personal desires that secretly exist do not hold potential harm. As such, you need to identify someone who can engage you in open conversations about this matter and the parameters to operate. Explore alternative avenues to satisfy these needs, such as self-pleasure, self-discovery, or engaging in spiritual nonsexual connections.

Finding Community:

A beneficial step is to seek out supportive communities as a single individual navigating a sexually charged environment. Connecting with like-minded individuals with similar values, interests, and perspectives opens an avenue to gain the necessary knowledge and skills. Within this community, one can seek to engage in social activities, join clubs or hobby groups, or attend workshops and classes. These approaches provide opportunities to meet new people and explore meaningful connections.

Being single in a sexually craved modern age may present unique challenges. But it also offers various opportunities for personal growth, self-discovery, and independence. Through redefining relationships, cultivating self-love, challenging societal pressures, navigating sexual cravings responsibly, and finding supportive communities, single individuals can confidently embrace solitude and create fulfilling lives on their terms.

Remember, being single does not equate to being incomplete. It is a chance to flourish, thrive, and discover the true essence of yourself.

LESSON SIXTEEN

Love Beyond Boundaries: Exploring The Phenomenon Of Same-Sex Marriage In Modern Age

Andrew and Ryan were a couple that lived in a quiet town called Louisville. They were a loving gay couple, deeply committed to each other and ready to embark on a journey together as husbands. However, their path was fraught with discrimination and stigma, challenging their love and resilience. Andrew and Ryan had been together for several years, nurturing a bond built on trust, respect, and shared dreams. They yearn for the day when they can exchange vows and declare their love to the world. Little did they know of the difficulties that lay ahead.

As they began planning their wedding, they faced disapproval from some conservative community members. Gossip whispered behind their backs, casting judgment and spreading hurtful rumours. The weight of discrimination clouded the couple's happiness, but they refused to let it extinguish their love. One day, while sitting under their favourite book tree, Andrew shared a personal experience with Ryan. He spoke of growing up in a household where his family did not accept his sexual orientation. Andrew's heartache was palpable, recounting the pain of feeling isolated, misunderstood, and rejected by his family. But he also spoke of resilience, of his finding a chosen family with the LGBTQ community, who had become their pillars of support.

Moved by Andrew's story, Ryan shared his struggles. He had faced discrimination at work, where colleagues made snide remarks and withheld opportunities due to his sexual orientation. Ryan spoke of the strength he found in his passion for advocacy, fighting for equal rights, and creating safe spaces for LGBTQ+ individuals. With their personal stories woven together, Andrew and Ryan face a daunting task: finding a venue to host their celebration. They encountered closed doors and rejection, but their determination remained unwavering.

Finally, they stumbled upon a kindhearted innkeeper who recognized their love as pure and beautiful. The innkeeper offered them a warm embrace, assuring them that their passion mattered and deserved the celebration. The wedding day arrived, and the town's rumours swirled. Many were skeptical, wondering if love could truly conquer discrimination. But as the ceremony unfolded, something magical happened.

The couple stood before their loved ones, exchanging heartfelt vows, their words resonating with authenticity and strength. Tears flowed freely, not just from Andrew and Ryan but from those who had doubted them. At that moment, prejudice began to crumble, replaced by a newfound understanding that love knows no boundaries.

From that day forward, Andrew and Ryan became symbols of resilience, love, and hope in the gay community. They continue to face discrimination, but they never let it define them. Instead, they used their personal experiences to educate, inspire, and create change. Their journey wasn't easy, but their love endured.

They overcame the stigma, one small victory at a time, by sharing their stories, offering support, and advocating for equality. Together, they taught their community that love is love and is worth celebrating in all its forms. And so, Andrew and Ryan, bound by love and strengthened by their shared experiences, lived happily thereafter, leaving behind a legacy of acceptance and compassion for generations to come.

In the modern age, humanity has made meaningful steps towards inclusivity and acceptance, evidently in the world of same-sex marriage. As things change and the world advances, so does our understanding and recognition of "love beyond traditional boundaries."

This lesson sheds some light, contradicting as it may appear, on the significance of same-sex marriage, highlighting its impact on individuals, communities, and society.

A Journey Towards Equality:

The journey towards recognizing same-sex marriage has seen many days of pain and sorrows, lack of safety and cruelty in its place, and tragedy betwixt defiance and triumph. Undoubtedly, it has been extended and laborious, marked by legal clashes, social stigma and discrimination, and personal struggles. However, the persistent efforts of LGBTQ+ activists and allies have paved the way for what many see as remarkable progress. Today, many countries have legalized same-sex marriage, acknowledging that love and commitment transcend gender.

Breaking Stereotypes And Challenging Prejudices:

Undoubtedly, same-sex marriage continues to challenge societal norms and stereotypes, which depict confined love to predefined roles. For many, all they see is that human relationships have broken free from the limitations that have hindered the collective growth of society. Same-sex couples exhibit love not confined by gender but as a universal force that unites individuals. Some express that it is high time that society embraces the diversity of human relationships, which will transform and allow for greater inclusion.

The Significance Of Marriage:

In the traditional and religious view, marriage is more than a legal contract; it is a celebration of love and commitment. Granting same-sex couples the right to marry provides them with legal protection and benefits and validates their relationship in the eyes of society. It allows them to experience the joys and accountabilities that come with the sacred foundation to foster stable and loving homes for families. Whether or not we are ready to accept this in its truest sense, this is what it means. The question is though, are we indeed there yet?

Benefits For Individuals, Communities, and Society:

Some groups within the society believe that recognizing same-sex marriage benefits individuals, communities, and society at large. Some people feel it promotes mental and emotional well-being within the LGBTQ+ community, as individuals no longer feel marginalized or excluded from any institution that symbolizes love and stability. Furthermore, they contend that same-sex marriage strengthens communities by encouraging inclusivity and acceptance, breaking down barriers, and promoting understanding.

Some discussions arise from the economic perspective that suggests that legalizing same-sex marriage has proven beneficial to some people. It stimulates local economies through increased spending on weddings, honeymoons, and related industries. What is certain is that freedom of movement has attracted tourists and is boosting the hospitality sector in some getaway destinations worldwide. This phenomenon occurs as more couples seek to choose destinations where their relationship is celebrated and respected.

Is This A Symbol Of Progress?

The debate has ended in some parts of the world and is to convene in other regions. Nonetheless, recognizing same-sex marriage is a testament to the advancement made as a society. Many still perceive this as a commitment to equality, justice, and respect for all. A powerful message is sent to future generations by embracing same-sex marriage: love knows no boundaries, and everyone deserves the same chance to build a life filled with happiness and contentment.

This modern age has revolutionized the recognition of same-sex marriage, representing a significant milestone in the ongoing pursuit of equality and acceptance. It has altered countless lives, crushed stereotypes, and heightened the fabric of our communities. As we continue to acknowledge and document love beyond traditional boundaries, people strive for a future where everyone, regardless of their sexual orientation, can experience the pleasures of a legally recognized union.

LESSON SEVENTEEN

Rediscovering The Sacred Bond: Exploring The Biblical Context Of Sex In Marriage

Sandra and David are a devout Christian couple. They have been married for several years and, like many other couples, have experienced the ups and downs of life. However, they felt something was missing in their marriage, a deep connection they longed to rediscover. One Sunday, as they sat in church listening to a sermon about love, respect, and the sacredness of marriage, Sandra's curiosity peaked. She turned to David and said, "Have you ever wondered about the biblical context of sex in marriage?" Surprised by the question, David replied, "Well, I suppose the bible does mention it, but we've never really explored it in depth. Why do you ask?" Sandra smiled gently and said, "I believe that understanding the sacredness of our physical union could help us deepen our bond and rediscover the beauty of our love. What if we embark on a journey to explore the biblical teachings and principles surrounding sex in marriage?"

Intrigued by Sandra's proposition, David agreed wholeheartedly. They began their quest by delving into scriptures, studying ancient texts, and seeking the wisdom of their pastor. They discovered that in the Bible, sex was not merely a physical act but a powerful expression of love, intimacy, and unity between a husband and wife. Guided by their newfound knowledge, Sandra and David intentionally changed their marriage. They started by setting aside time for prayer and reflection, asking for God's guidance in their intimate relationship. They renewed their commitment to each other, promising to honour and cherish their sacred bond.

As they grew closer spiritually, they also sought to understand each other's desires and needs. They began communicating more openly, sharing their hopes, fears, and dreams. They discovered that true intimacy was not just about physical pleasure but also emotional and spiritual connection. With newfound passion and a renewed sense of purpose, Sandra and David began exploring their relationship's physical aspects. They discovered that the bible celebrated the joy and pleasure that sex could bring within the boundaries of marriage. They embraced this understanding, allowing themselves to experience the happiness and delight God had intended for them.

Over time, their love deepened, and their bond grew stronger. Their newfound knowledge of the biblical context of sex in marriage reignited their passion and brought them closer to God and each other. Sandra and David became an inspiration to others in their church community. They shared their journey with fellow couples, encouraging them to explore the sacredness of their marital union.

They organized workshops, led bible studies, and mentored those who sought guidance. Their once-faltering marriage had been a testament to God's love and grace. Sandra and David realized that true intimacy was not something to be ashamed of or hidden away. Instead, it was a beautiful gift from God to celebrate and cherish.

Ultimately, Sandra and David's journey taught them that the sacred bond between a husband and wife reflected Christ and his church's divine love and unity. They understood that their love, rooted in faith and guided by biblical principles, could flourish and become a source of joy, strength, and inspiration to all those around them.

In this modern era, where cultural norms and values are rapidly evolving, it is essential to reflect on the timeless wisdom and guidance provided by the bible. One aspect that often arouses interest and discussion is the biblical framework of sex within the sacred institution of marriage. As society grapples with shifting attitudes towards sexuality, it is central to understand the biblical principles that underpin the sacredness of sex in marriage.

God's Design For Marital Intimacy:

In various accounts, the bible asserts that God created sex as a gift within the bond of marriage. This marriage, however, refers to a man and woman in the union, which always will be a discussion even regarding same-sex marriage. Genesis 2:24 states, "Therefore, a man shall leave his father and his mother and hold fast to his wife, and they shall become one flesh." This verse highlights the profound union that occurs when a man and a woman come together in marriage, physically, emotionally, and spiritually. It emphasizes the exclusivity and obligation required to experience the fullness of such a sacred bond.

Mutual Love And Respect:

There is a particular emphasis in the bible on the importance of love and respect within a marital relationship. As revealed in Ephesians 5:25, the scriptures state, "Husbands, love your wives, as Christ loved the church and gave himself up for her." This verse admonishes husbands to love and honour their wives selflessly. In a similar context, 2 Corinthian 7:3-4 encourages mutual respect, stating that both partners have authority over each other's bodies, stressing the need for consent and equivalence in sexual intimacy.

The Role Of Pleasure And Intimacy:

Contrary to some popular misconceptions, the bible celebrates the enjoyment and pleasure of sexual intimacy within marriage. The song of Solomon beautifully depicts the passionate and intimate love between a husband and a wife. This lesson showcases the beauty of sexual desire and the importance of expressing it within the boundaries of a committed relationship.

Fidelity And Exclusivity:

The Bible consistently emphasizes the excellent value and importance of fidelity and exclusivity in the marital relationship. Hebrews 13:4 compounds it by concluding, "Let marriage be held in honour among all, and let the marriage bed be undefiled." While this verse underscores the need for faithfulness and the sanctity of the marital bond, it does not stop people from performing such acts as open relationships where partners can see other people; threesome sexual encounters; and double families where men have more than one wife with children. Through the Christian doctrine, God encourages couples to find fulfillment, satisfaction, and intimacy within their relationship rather than seeking it outside marriage.

Deep Conversation And Meaning In Intimacy:

Even the bible takes a stance regarding open and honest communication to foster a healthy relationship within the confines of marriage. 1 Corinthians 7:5 advises couples not to deprive each other of sexual intimacy, except by mutual agreement, to avoid temptation and discord. This bible passage unequivocally underscores the importance of having deep conversations and meaning of each other's needs, desires, and boundaries. It guides how to nurture a durable and satisfying sexual bond.

When individuals garner a complete understanding of the biblical context of sex in marriage, it gives rise to better direction and foundation on which to navigate the complications of modern relationships. It emphasizes the core tenets of a good, administered relationship, including fidelity, mutual respect, love, and communication within the sacred union of marriage. Without a doubt, this modern-era society often trivializes or distorts the significance of sexual intimacy.

Re-experiencing the biblical principles can help couples embrace this gift's true beauty and sacredness. Couples can nurture a deep, fulfilling, and lasting bond when these principles are honoured. Through this type of bond, they can truly experience the profound union God designed within the sacred institution of marriage.

Biblical Views Of Gay Marriage And Intimacy

The topic of gay marriage and intimacy within a biblical context is a wide debate and various religious denominations and scholars interpret it differently. It is important to note that perspectives on this issue can vary and may not represent the views of all individuals or religious groups. Some interpret specific passages in the bible as explicitly condemning same-sex relationships and consider them sinful. For example, in the Old Testament, Leviticus 18:22 states, "You shall not lie with a male as with a woman; it is an abomination." Similarly, in the New Testament, 1 Corinthians 6: 9-10 mentions that: "men who have sex with men" will not inherit the Kingdom of God.

However, some scholars believe it is vital to approach biblical interpretation with an understanding of the historical and cultural context in which these texts were written. Scholars argue that these verses may have addressed specific situations, such as temple prostitution or sexual exploitation, rather than condemning all same-sex relationships.

Other biblical scholars and religious groups emphasize the importance of love, inclusion, and acceptance for all individuals, regardless of sexual orientation. They argue that the overarching message of the Bible is one of love and compassion and that the focus should be on treating others with respect and dignity.

In recent years, some religious denominations have become more accepting of gay marriage and intimacy. They interpret biblical teachings through a lens of love, equality, and the belief that God can bless committed same-sex relationships. Ultimately, interpretations of the bible on this topic differ, and it is up to individuals and religious communities to establish a spiritual connection with God to gain a greater understanding based on their beliefs and values. It is essential to approach discussion surrounding this issue with empathy, respect, and an open mind.

LESSON EIGHTEEN

When Love Is Not Enough: Directing The Next Steps

Jacob, a 37-year-old man, had many intimate partner experiences throughout his young life. He consciously decided to navigate his future when love was not enough. Jacob was a kindhearted and compassionate man who was always willing to lend a helping hand to those who needed help. Jacob himself had many dreams and aspirations, a clear vision for his future. However, he seemed to attract intimate partners who lacked direction, causing him to face tremendous challenges.

Jacob's first love, Angela, was a free-spirited artist who lived in the moment. While Jacob admired her creativity and zest for life, he soon realized that her lack of low focus hindered their shared vision for the future. They would often get lost in passionate discussions and grand ideas, but Angela had trouble committing when it came to taking practical steps toward their dreams. Eventually, their relationship crumbled under the weight of unfulfilled promises.

Heartbroken but determined, Jacob picked up the pieces of his shattered dreams and carried on. He met Sierra, a successful businesswoman who seemed to have it all figured out. Sierra was ambitious and driven, always striving for success. Jacob found solace in her stability and envied her unwavering focus. However, as time passed, he discovered that a severe obsession with her career left little room for emotional connection. Their relationship became a mere transaction, devoid of the love and support he craved.

Undeterred, Jacob refused to lose faith in finding a partner who shared his desires for a balanced and fulfilling life. He met Lily, a compassionate and caring woman who dreams of making a difference. They connected deeply, and Jacob saw in her the potential for a life full of love and purpose. But as the relationship progressed, Jacob noticed that Lily's commitment to her cause often precedes their connection—her determination to make a difference left little room for the relationship to thrive.

Exhausted from navigating the challenges of love, Jacob found himself at a crossroads. He realized that love alone was insufficient to sustain a fulfilling and purposeful life. He needed a partner who shared his dreams and possessed the drive and focus to turn those dreams into reality.

With newfound clarity, Jacob embarked on a journey of self-discovery. He embraced his passions and dedicated himself to personal growth. He surrounded himself with like-minded individuals who shared his values and aspirations. Through this process, Jacob learned that his happiness and fulfillment depended not solely on finding the right partner but on creating a life aligned with his deepest desires.

Years went by, and Jacob's resilience paid off. He met Rebecca, a woman with the perfect balance of passion and focus. Rebecca was an artist like Angela, successful like Sierra, and passionate like Lily. She shared Jacob's vision for the future, and together, they embarked on a journey of love, growth, and purpose.

Jacob had learned that love alone was not enough to navigate life's challenges. It required a partner who shared his drive, ambition, and commitment to personal growth. With Rebecca by his side, they turned their dreams into his desired reality, supporting each other through triumphs and failures. They understood that love was the foundation, but their shared purpose propelled them to conquer any obstacles that came their way.

Jacob's story became a testament to the fact that when love is not enough, finding a partner who aligns with your goals and values can create a life that is truly extraordinary. Never be afraid to venture out alone, as everything will fall into place when the time is right. When love is not enough, know it needs a greater sense of understanding and belonging. And when you take this journey alone and discover all the things you have, you will recognize when it demands more than just love but understanding and satisfaction as the way forward.

Love is undoubtedly a powerful force that can unite two people, but what happens when love alone is not enough to sustain a relationship? Relationships are complex and require more than love to thrive. When faced with this realization, exploring the following steps to chart the way ahead becomes essential.

There will be times regardless of your best efforts, your relationships cannot survive. So here comes the crossroad that you have dreaded for a long time. In this lesson, we will explore how communication among other chapters in life can be a much-needed solution. Herein lies the steps necessary to move beyond this roadblock.

One of the first steps that one must take to ensure that relationship issues go on the table for decisions, must be honest and open communication. Again and again, communication will continue to dominate this book as an essential action step in establishing and maintaining relationships. It is no secret that it is the foundation of any successful relationship. When love is not enough, having a thoughtful and sincere conversation with your partner is fundamental, ironing out challenges foreseen and difficulties charting the way ahead. Express your concerns, fears, and doubts while actively listening to their perspectives. This dialogue can uncover underlying issues and help determine if the relationship can evolve and thrive or if the best decision is to part peacefully.

Self-Reflection:

Often, when love is not enough in a relationship, people tend to look at the opposite partner, but instead, self-reflection is necessary. Before making any decisions, it is crucial to engage in self-reflection. This act will reveal to us our tolerance level or our flaws and, indeed, our limitations. We must ask ourselves some questions: "Do I have unresolved conflicts that will hinder or prevent this relationship from going forward? Are there unmet needs or a lack of compatibility? Understanding your feelings and needs will undoubtedly enable you to make more informed choices about the future and your desires as you navigate future relationships.

Who Will Hold My Hands:

Sometimes, having a neutral third party that can provide you with the valuable insights and guidance needed is crucial. It is also wise to consider seeking the help of a couple's therapist or relationship counsellor, as these individuals train to see beyond what we can see. These professionals train to help couples navigate complex emotions and communication barriers and offer tools to work through challenges. Therapy can also provide a safe space to explore deeper issues and help to determine if there is a way forward.

Re-evaluating Expectations:

Often, when love is not enough, it is because our expectations are not aligned. It is, therefore, essential to take the time to reevaluate what you want and the needs that you think you have derived from a relationship. From assessing your expectations, we'll examine whether there are realistic expectations and if a compromise is possible. It may also be necessary to adjust or simply accept that your goals may not be compatible or aligned with your partners.

Is Personal Growth My Answer:

Sometimes, it is that the next step when love is not enough is to focus on personal growth. These are the opportune times to invest in self-improvement, self-care, and pursuing individual interests that could also be factors that have been holding you back from giving all of you to someone else. This period of self-discovery can help you clarify what you truly desire in a relationship and whether staying together is the best choice for either partner.

Considering A Break Or Separation:

Taking a break or temporary separation can offer both partners the space to assess the relationship more objectively. Time spent apart will help put things in perspective and allow you to weigh the pros and cons of being in a relationship or being out of it. This time apart can provide valuable insights into whether the issue is being resolved and if the love shared is strong enough to withstand future challenges.

What's Next, Accept And Move On:

Sometimes, despite your best efforts, love may not be enough to sustain the relationship. It may be time to accept that this relationship will not work and thus move on. Acceptance can be difficult, I'm sure, but it is often the healthiest choice for both individuals involved. Understand that sometimes, love alone cannot overcome fundamental differences or even compatible goals.

When love is not enough, it is essential to take proactive steps to evaluate the situation, communicate openly, and seek professional help if necessary. Whether it leads to growth, compromise, or moving on, remember that love is just one aspect of our relationships. There will be many more opportunities to decide where you go with your life, what you can tolerate, and what you can withstand. At this point, you evaluate and determine if there are other factors to consider for long-term happiness and fulfillment.

LESSON NINETEEN

Unmasking Reality: A Critical Examination Of Sexual And Intimate Violence In Today's Society

There was a 35-year-old woman, Victoria. Victoria was a kindhearted soul who possessed immense strength despite living in a marriage that caused her unimaginable grief and pain. Behind closed doors, her husband Joseph subjected her to constant abuse and treated her like an object rather than a human being. Victoria's days were filled with fear and anxiety, never knowing when the next outburst would occur. The violence was physical and extended in their intimate moments, where Joseph would force himself upon her, leaving her feeling violated and broken. Each instance chipped away at her self-worth, leaving her feeling trapped and suffocated, lost within the confines of her own home.

Victoria's spirit began to wither as time passed, and the once vibrant light within her dimmed. Yet, deep inside her heart, a tiny flicker of hope remained. She knew that she deserved better and was worthy of love and respect. This glimmer of courage eventually gave her the strength to seek help and escape the clutches of her tormentor. One day, Victoria stumbled upon a local support group for survivors of domestic violence. In the sacred space, she found solace among individuals who have endured similar experiences. They shared stories of strength, resilience, and the journey towards healing. Victoria's heart opened, and she realized she was not alone.

Encouraged by the empathy and understanding she found within the support group, Victoria began to formulate an escape plan. She confided in trusted friends and family members, who rallied around her, offering their unwavering support. Together, they ensured her safety and devised a strategy that would allow her to leave the toxic environment she had endured for far too long.

On a moonless night, when the darkness embraced the world, Victoria summoned every ounce of her courage and made her escape. She left the pain and abuse behind, stepping into a new chapter of her life, one filled with hope and possibilities. The road ahead was uncertain, but Victoria was determined to reclaim her life and rediscover her worth.

With the support of local organizations dedicated to helping survivors, Victoria found a haven where she could begin her healing journey. She attended counselling sessions, engaged in empowering activities, and surrounded herself with individuals who nurtured her spirit.

Slowly, she rebuilt the shattered pieces of her self-esteem, finding strength in her resilience and the knowledge that she had escaped the clutches of her abuser. Victoria's bruised heart began to heal as time passed, and her spirit grew more robust. She became an advocate for survivors of domestic violence, using her voice to raise awareness and empower others to break free from their prisons of abuse.

Victoria's story inspired those who believed they were trapped, reminding them there is always hope and a way out. With each step she took towards healing, Victoria transformed her pain into purpose. She vowed to make a difference and be a beacon of light for those trapped in the darkness. Through her resilience and unwavering courage, Victoria showed the world that even in the face of unimaginable adversity, there is always the possibility of finding freedom and reclaiming one's life.

Sexual intimate violence continues to be a prevalent and distressful global societal issue. It violates fundamental human rights, enabling fear, trauma, and inequality cycles. This lesson, therefore, aims to shed light on the dark reality of sexual and intimate partner violence. This section will critically examine prevalence, featuring causes and the need for urgent and complete action.

Through the lens of the victims:

Intimate partner violence is commonly known as domestic violence, a cowardly act in which one partner acts violently towards another.

Intimate partner violence is a worldwide phenomenon and encompasses violence of a psychological, physical, sexual, and emotional nature perpetrated by an intimate partner. For victims of intimate partner violence, the experience can be incredibly traumatic and life-altering. The effect of this violence extends way beyond the actual incidents of abuse. It infiltrates every aspect of a victim's life and causes profound emotional and physical damage. Let us examine the various components of affect for victims.

Physically, victims may bear the scars and bruises from the many violent encounters. As this physical evidence presents itself, the endurance of pain and suffering resulting from the abuse also lies. These injuries can range from mild to severe, sometimes leading to long-term health conditions and even death in extreme cases. Fear of physical harm often causes victims to be on edge, constantly living in anxiety and hypervigilance.

Emotionally, victims of intimate partner violence often experience a range of complex and conflicting emotions. They often feel trapped, isolated, and hopeless and firmly believe they cannot escape their abusive partner. The constant emotional manipulation, degrading, and control inflicted upon them can erode their self-esteem, self-confidence, and self-worth, leaving them powerless and incapable of breaking free.

Psychologically, victims suffer from various mental health conditions due to abuse. Depression, anxiety, post-traumatic stress disorder (PTSD), and suicidal ideation are just some of the examples of the psychological toll taken on victims. Again, the constant fear is driven in these people by their abuser. These insecurities often lead to perpetual trauma, making life challenging for victims to regain a sense of normalcy and stability in their lives.

Beyond the physical, emotional, and psychological impact, intimate partner violence also affects victims socially and economically. Their relationships with family and friends may also become strained and sometimes severed due to either their abuser's manipulation and isolation tactics or the embarrassment and shame they fear showing. Victims may also face financial hardships, as their abusers exert control over the finances or withhold money from their access. In this setting, the abused partner has little or no means or access to the resources necessary to leave the relationship.

It is crucial to recognize that intimate partner violence is not limited to just persons in the lower socioeconomic class of society, gender, age, or ethnic groups. Victims come from all walks of life. Breaking the cycle of abuse requires a collective effort from society, including advocacy, education, and support services. Ultimately, intimate partner violence through the lens of the victim is a harrowing experience that leaves lasting scars on every aspect of life.

Therefore, society must raise awareness, cultivate empathy, and provide the needed resources to empower victims to break free from the unhealthy cycle of abuse and rebuild their lives.

Frequency And Under Reporting In The Matter:

It is disheartening to acknowledge that sexual and intimate partner violence remains alarmingly prevalent in many societies across the globe. The records continue to note countless victims, mainly women, silently bearing the burden of their distressing experiences due to fear, shame, and societal stigmas. The World Health Organization estimates that nearly one in three women will experience sexual or intimate partner violence during their lifetime. Moreover, we are also seeing more recently that men and members of the LGBTQ+ community are becoming victims of such violence. These shortcomings further highlight the urgency to address this issue holistically.

Root Causes And Societal Factors:

Sexual and intimate partner violence is somehow profoundly entrenched in power inequalities, gender disparity, and cultural norms that prolong destructive behaviours. Male-controlled structures in many parts of the world often prioritize the dominance of men, leading to the objectification and downgrading of women. The demonic act of objectifying women, combined with societal pressures, contributes to the blaming of victims. Without a doubt, this act further silences many survivors and prolongs a culture of violence. Sadly, while there have been remarkable headways in technology, the media, including pornography, also plays a role in reinforcing harmful narratives. To honestly examine the narratives, the results, often, normalize aggression and distort the very perceptions of things such as consent and choice.

The Role Of Education And Awareness:

The key to intimate partner violence lies heavily in the education of fundamental human rights and justice. The downplaying of education is evident on many avenues in the conversation of violence in general. Education and awareness play a pivotal role in fighting sexual and intimate partner violence and should be in unison and one accord. Hence, there is a need for comprehensive sex education programs to be implemented at an early age, promoting healthy relationships and consent and including values and respect components.

By addressing the root causes through education, individuals can understand the importance of consent, boundaries, and equality. Raising awareness through media campaigns, community activities and initiatives, and public discourse can help challenge societal norms and break the cycle of violence.

The Voice Of Legal And Policy Reforms:

In the mix of all the arguments, adequate legal frameworks and policies are required and deemed urgent to combat sexual and intimate partner violence. Governments must ensure survivors access justice, protection, and support systems. Strengthening laws against sexual assault, harassment, and domestic violence and providing adequate resources for survivors is required. Encouragingly, some countries have made significant progress in this area, but more needs to happen to ensure consistent global action.

Strengthening Survivors And Crushing The Silence:

As we explore this critical subject, we conclude that strengthening survivors is paramount in the fight against sexual and intimate partner violence. Organizations and helplines should readily offer counselling, medical assistance, and legal guidance. Creating safe spaces where survivors can share their experiences without judgment is essential for their healing process. It is crucial that society actively listens to survivors, believes their stories, and takes collective responsibility to eradicate the culture of violence.

While sex and sexuality embrace so many sweet, lasting, and intriguing facets of our lives and existence, sexual and intimate violence remains deeply ingrained in our society, necessitating urgent and comprehensive action. Through education, awareness, legal reforms, and support for survivors, we can work towards dismantling the societal structures that enable such violence. Together, we can foster a culture that respects consent, promotes equality, and ensures the safety and dignity of every individual. Let us unite in our communities and our commitment to bringing an end to sexual and intimate partner violence.

LESSON TWENTY

Rekindling Passion: Sexual Intimacy For Seniors In Today's Modern Society

Once upon a time, the charming senior couple named Henry and Margaret lived in a quiet town nestled among the rolling hills. They had been married for over six decades, and their love had only grown stronger with time. As they gracefully aged, they discovered new and beautiful ways to embrace romance and intimacy. Henry would wake up early every morning and prepare a sumptuous breakfast for Margaret. He would carefully arrange fresh fruits, warm pastries, and a cup of fragrant coffee. With her silver hair neatly combed and twinkled green eyes, Margaret would save her every bite, feeling the love Henry poured into each meal.

In the evenings, they would take strolls hand in hand, exploring the charming streets of their town. They would pause to admire the blooming flowers and hear the birds serenade them with their melodious song. With each step, they revelled in the shared joy of simply being together, finding comfort and solace in the familiar touch of their intertwined fingers. Henry and Margaret would embark on small adventures on weekends, visiting nearby parks or lakes. They would pack a picnic basket filled with their favourite snacks and a bottle of wine. Sitting on a cozy blanket, they would reminisce about their youth, sharing stories of their early years and laughing at their misadventures. Through their conversations and laughter, they built a bridge between the past and present, further cementing their bond.

At sunset, they would return home, where they transformed their living room into a dance floor. With a twinkle in his eyes, Henry would gently take Margaret in his arms, and they would sway to the rhythmic melodies of their favourite old songs. Their bodies may have grown frail, but their hearts danced with the same enthusiasm as when they were young. They whispered promises of love and devotion with every step, cherishing each moment as if it were their last. Their romance extended far beyond the physical realms. They found intimacy in gestures, like holding hands while watching their favourite movies, sharing secrets over cups of tea, or leaving love notes for each other to discover. Every night before drifting off to sleep, they would lie side by side, their hands entwined, and talk about their dreams, fears, and hopes. They were each other's confidants, their love, a haven in a tumultuous world.

Their love for one another deepened as the years passed and their bodies aged. They taught the world that intimacy and romance were not confined to youth but could flourish and blossom with age. Their story inspired everyone who witnessed their love, reminding them that love knows no boundaries and that true intimacy lies in the moments shared between two souls who have weathered life storms together. Henry and Margaret continued to embrace their love, cherishing every moment they had left on this earth. They became a witness to the power of love, proving that with age comes wisdom, and with knowledge comes a profound understanding of what truly matters - the enduring connection between two hearts that beats in harmony until the end of time.

In today's modern society, there is a growing recognition of the importance of sexual intimacy among seniors, even those in retirement. Their consideration is vital with increased expectations that people will live longer, especially with improved health. We are witnessing individuals who are embracing their latter years with a desire to maintain fulfilling relationships and satisfying sexual lives.

This lesson aims to shed light on the importance of sexual intimacy for seniors, their challenges, and how society can support and encourage this aspect of their lives.

Traditionally, discussions surrounding sexuality and aging have been considered taboo, often leading to a lack of acknowledgment or support for seniors' sexual needs. However, contemporary society is witnessing a shift in attitudes, recognizing that sexual intimacy is a natural and healthy part of life, irrespective of age. By challenging stereotypes and promoting open dialogue, we can create a more inclusive and understanding environment for seniors seeking sexual fulfillment.

Whether we are ready for this or not, engaging in sexual activity has various health benefits for seniors. It can improve cardiovascular health, reduce stress levels, boost immune systems, and increase overall well-being. Additionally, sexual intimacy releases endorphins, which act as natural pain relievers and can help alleviate symptoms of chronic conditions such as arthritis. By understanding and promoting these benefits, society can encourage seniors to embrace their sexual identities and enhance their quality of life.

Managing And Addressing Physical And Emotional Challenges:

Seniors, like individuals of any age, can face various physical and emotional challenges regarding intimacy. These challenges may vary from person to person, but some things happen daily among most people. The evidence shows that physical limitations are inevitable for aging and seniors. Seniors may experience material changes that can affect their comfort level and ability to engage in intimacy. There are some conditions, such as arthritis, limited mobility, chronic pain, or illnesses, that can impact their physical capabilities, making certain activities more challenging.

A second factor is the hormonal changes that will be debilitating to seniors. As people age, many changes can occur, often affecting libido and sexual desires. Both men and women may experience decreased sex hormones, reduced interest in intimacy, or changes in their sexual functioning. Then there are the mental and emotional concerns. Seniors may face emotional challenges related to the whole intimacy prospect. These dynamic challenges connect to self-esteem issues, body image concerns, or primary anxiety. These feelings are often influenced by societal stereotypes and age-related insecurities, which can impact their willingness to engage in intimate relationships, regardless of who feels they need to live such a life.

Then, there is the concern of the loss of a partner. Many seniors have experienced the loss of a long-term partner or spouse, so coping with grief and the emotional aftermath of losing someone they are close to can make it difficult to reestablish intimacy or establish new relationships. Nonetheless, others will choose to start all over and build intimate relationships. However, they may not be able to reach their full potential because of the loss they have experienced. Some may have grown up in a time when discussing topics related to intimacy and sexual health was considered taboo. As a result, they may lack proper education, information, or resources regarding maintaining healthy sexual relationships as they age. With this mindset, they may settle on not engaging or getting involved and continue to live lonely lives.

It is important to note that seniors have diverse experiences and preferences regarding intimacy. Nevertheless, some may have alternative ways to express intimacy, while others prioritize emotional connections over physical ones. Although the desire and libido are partially functional, open communication, understanding, and seeking support from healthcare professionals or groups can help seniors navigate these challenges and maintain fulfilling and intimate lives.

Supporting Healthy Relationships:

Maintaining a supportive, healthy, intimate relationship can be a fulfilling and beautiful experience as a senior. Communicate our needs, desires, and concerns with our partners, which are essential. In all our endeavours, we must listen actively and empathize with our partners and feelings. This kind of connection is what is necessary at this unique life stage. Prioritizing our physical and emotional well-being plays an important part. An exemplary component of this is eating well, doing regular exercises, and maintaining regular medical checkups with your healthcare provider. Also, try to be emotionally supportive, understand each other's needs, and provide comfort and reassurance when necessary.

We must embrace intimacy, as it comes in many different forms, not just physical. Giving emotional intimacy is equally important, so we need to look at spending quality time together, engaging in activities we enjoy, and sharing our thoughts and feelings openly. Physical intimacy can also be a part of this so we can discuss any concerns or challenges we may experience with our partners. It is good to explore new ways to connect that are comfortable and pleasurable for both of us.

Keep the romance alive, and by doing so, we surprise each other with small gestures of affection, like leaving love notes or planning surprises. Continue to date and explore new experiences together. It is essential to nurture the romantic aspects of our relationship to keep this spark alive. We sometimes need to adapt to the changes together. As we age, our bodies and circumstances change. We must be patient and understanding with each other as we adapt to these changes. We also must be mindful of new ways of connecting and adjusting to potential limitations.

It is always wise to remember that seeking support when needed can be reassuring. If, for any reason, challenges arise or we feel stuck, don't hesitate to seek professional help. Again, couples therapy or counselling can provide guidance and tools to navigate any difficulties that we may encounter. Every relationship is unique, so finding what works best for us and our partners is essential. So, we always seek open communication and mutual respect to strengthen our commitment to each other's well-being. As seniors, we must always strive to maintain a supportive, healthy, and fulfilling intimate relationship.

Accepting Technology And Education:

Technology and education can be invaluable tools in supporting sexual intimacy among seniors. Online resources, educational workshops, and support groups can provide information on sexual health, relationship advice, and techniques to enhance intimacy. Additionally, technological advancements such as sex toys designed for seniors can aid in overcoming physical challenges and promote sexual satisfaction. With the support of these tools, seniors can explore new avenues of pleasure and maintain fulfilling sexual lives.

LESSON TWENTY-ONE

Navigating Sexual Intimacy: A Guide For Today's Youth

Emily was a young adolescent living in a tranquil town with her dad and stepmom. She was a curious and free-spirited beauty, eagerly embracing the world with open arms. As Emily entered her teenage years, her curiosity wandered into sexual intimacy, a path that would prove challenging and enlightening. Emily's journey began with innocent curiosity as she sought to understand the nuances of human connection and the mystery of desire. She embarked on a quest for knowledge, devouring books, social media posts, and articles, hoping to gain insights into this realm that felt simultaneously enticing and intimidating.

However, Emily soon realized that crossing the world of sexual intimacy was not as straightforward as she had imagined. She encountered societal expectations, rigid stereotypes, and conflicting messages that left her feeling confused and uncertain. Faced with these challenges, she felt shame and self-doubt creeping into her mind. But Emily was determined not to let these obstacles deter her. She sought guidance from trusted individuals who could provide a safe space for her to express her concerns and share her experiences. A compassionate counsellor became her confidant, offering advice and helping her discern the difference between healthy exploration and harmful behaviours.

As Emily continued her journey, she discovered that communication was vital to building healthy relationships. She learned the relevance of embracing open and honest conversations with partners expressing personal desires, boundaries, and concerns. In doing so, Emily found strength in her vulnerability and discovered the power of consent. Abstinence was a big thing for her, and she found there was more than one way to express how she felt with people she built intimate relationships with. She explored new avenues on how to remain relevant during these times.

Emily's path was not without its setbacks. There were moments when she encountered heartbreaks, betrayal, and disappointments. Yet, she refused to let these experiences define her. Instead, she used them as opportunities for growth and self-reflection, alternately emerging stronger and wiser. Through her struggles, Emily also uncovered moments of intense joy and connection. She experienced the tender touch of her partner, who respected her boundaries, the warmth of a shared laugh during intimate moments, and the blissful contentment of feeling indeed seen and accepted.

As Emily matured, she realized that her journey was not a destination but an ongoing process of self-discovery. She understood that sexual intimacy was a deep, personal, unique experience for every individual and that there was no "right" or "wrong" way to navigate it. With time, Emily became a green light for others embarking on similar journeys. She shared her stories of challenges and successes with her peers, offering guidance and support to those who needed it. She advocated for open conversations about sexual health and consent to create a world where other adolescents could explore intimacy with confidence and respect.

Finally, Emily's path intertwined with the lives of countless others, leaving a lasting impact on her community. Her journey taught her that the road to understanding sexual intimacy was not always smooth, but it was worth taking. It was a journey of self-discovery, empowerment, and growth that allowed her to embrace her desires and navigate the complexities of human connection with grace and compassion.

In today's rapidly evolving society, there is great urgency for discussions around sexual intimacy, especially for today's youth. Navigating sexual intimacy as a youth is essential and challenging daily; making the right decision and facing modern dilemmas have become increasingly important. With the internet, social media, and easy access to information, it is crucial to provide young people with comprehensive knowledge and guidance in navigating their journey of sexual intimacy.

This lesson will speak directly to youths to shed light on various aspects of sexual intimacy. This discussion includes consent, communication, safety, and emotional well-being to empower and educate young individuals as they embark on this significant aspect of life.

My Advice To You Innocents:

As you embark on this sexually intimate journey, always put this phrase at the front of your mind: "Knowledge is power." It will help you inform yourself of your decisions and assure you that you will feel more confident in intimate relationships. An essential part of managing sexual intimacy is to trust your instincts. Trusting your instincts and listening to your body and emotions is a guiding light, even in the dark. Still, be careful and always remember that you have a choice. You are the one that determines the pace at which you move toward the act of sex and commitment in relationships. If something doesn't feel fitting or comfortable, speaking up and advocating for yourself is essential.

Consider the wise counsel of family, adults, and professional counsellors or relationship coaches. It also does not hurt to get advice and guidance from educators, healthcare providers, trusted friends, or peers with experience in this area. Having someone to talk to and share experiences with can offer valuable insights and support. If you feel overwhelmed or unsure, it is always a good habit to step away from the pressure you are feeling and recoup.

Always remember to move strategically and purposefully. Intimate partners will force you to engage in deep penetrating sexual activities, and you must go into that situation adequately prepared. Take it at your own pace, and remember that everyone develops physically and emotionally differently. People feel different things at various times. It is okay to explore sexual intimacy at a rate that feels comfortable for you. Don't rush into anything; ensure you are ready and willing when the time comes.

Always remember that consent is crucial in any sexual experience. It should always be enthusiastic, ongoing, and mutual with whoever you are in an intimate relationship with. While you seek respect from your partner, you must also set your boundaries and ensure they respect yours. Consensual and respectful interactions are the foundations of a healthy sexual relationship. You must also take the time to educate yourself about sexual health, consent, contraception, and safe sex practices.

Why The Need For Consent And Communication:

Consent is the foundation of any healthy sexual relationship. Understanding that consent must be enthusiastic, ongoing, and given without coercion or pressure is crucial. The education system should educate young people about the significance of obtaining explicit and affirmative consent from their partners before engaging in sexual activity. Emphasizing that consent can be withdrawn at any time is essential to fostering a culture of respect and ensuring mutual enjoyment.

Open, honest communication is vital for fulfilling sexual experiences. Young individuals should feel comfortable discussing their desires, boundaries, and concerns with their partner. Encouraging conversations about likes, dislikes, and expectations can establish trust and intimacy, leading to a more enjoyable experience.

Safe Sex Practices:

Safe sex practices are essential for everyone and, more so, especially for today's youth as they seek to navigate the sexual and intimate world. For a child to become aware of safe sex practices, being well-informed and educated is important. The information and education about sexually transmitted infections (STIs) and unintended pregnancies will protect them and their partners. Help me to examine these safe sex practices that all youth should be aware of to protect themselves.

1. **Consistent Condom Use**: condoms are one of the most effective barrier methods against transmitting sexually transmitted infections, including HIV. The health authorities recommend using a condom during sex correctly and consistently. Whether their sexual action is vaginal, anal, or oral sexual activities, use a barrier method. The options of barrier methods can be a condom or a dental dam. The latter is a piece of latex rubber material cut in a squared shape that is stretched by both hands and placed over the vagina or anus. It is made from the same latex material as condoms, or use a regular condom when cut open. They are barrier methods because they provide a physical barrier against STIs and help prevent unplanned pregnancies.

2. **Regular STI Testing:** Getting tested for STIs regularly is crucial, even if you do not have any symptoms. Many STIs may not even show up immediately but can transmit to sexual partners. Regular testing ensures early detection and timely treatment.

3. **Open Honest Conversation**: I am confident you would have seen in every section of this book that a focal point addresses open and honest communication. It ensures that every reader knows this concept's importance and core relevance. Discussing sexual histories, STI testing, and contraception

methods helps make informed decisions and maintain a healthy sexual relationship. It means that you are in the know with your partner, where they have been, with whom, what their intentions were previously and presently for you, and their behaviours and practices. This way, you are guaranteed awareness and knowledge to make informed decisions to move ahead safely.

4. **Birth Control Methods:** When engaging in sexual activities that could lead to pregnancy, exploring and using reliable birth control methods is crucial. For you to do so, it is best to consult a healthcare professional to discuss your options, such as oral contraceptives, intrauterine devices (IUDs), implants, patches, and condoms combined with other methods. There are various brands, so selection should not be too difficult.

5. **Limiting The Number Of Sexual Partners:** When you reduce the number of sexual partners that you have, it lowers the risk of exposure to STIs. It undoubtedly puts you in a better position to trace issues that may arise while it offers you better protection from STIs and mishaps with pregnancy. Indeed, you can see how multiple sex partners in pregnancy situations can result in complications or accidents of children given to the wrong father. Moreover, if numerous sexual partners are

involved, it is even more important to practice safe sex and get tested regularly.

6. **Vaccinations:** In some countries, vaccination is an option. Vaccines such as the HPV vaccine are available to protect against certain STIs. It is wise to consult a healthcare professional to understand recommended vaccines. Always remember that your sexual health is a personal responsibility, and when you practice safe sex, it is essential for your overall well-being.

For you to stay well in general, you must stay informed. Always discuss the issues and have concise conversations about them. Of course, the final decision should be to seek help and support from healthcare professionals, who can provide more accurate information and support for this journey and maintain a healthy sexual life.

Emotional Well-Being:

Sexual intimacy is not only about the physical aspect but also about emotional connection. When it comes to the engagement of sexual activity, youths need to be aware of and prioritize their emotional well-being. It is so cliché that humans, in general, engaging in any form of sexual activity can bring about a range of complex emotions. Understanding and addressing these emotions is essential for a healthy and positive experience. Emotional well-being starts with consent and open communication. In most situations, when adequate discussions do not occur before the sexual encounter, individuals feel less of a person or a sense of being cheapened.

It is vital to establish clear boundaries and ensure that both partners, as youthful as they may be, come to a consensus and are comfortable and enthusiastic about their engagement in this sexual activity. Similarly, the conversation should focus on each person's desires, limits, and expectations that they can experience during and after the sexual encounter. The *"slam bam, thank you, mam"* is no longer it. The youth now say it is who first "cum" (climax) wins!!! For many, there is no tolerance after one partner reaches their satisfaction level and abruptly ends the encounter. Violence often erupts at this point. Such conversation can help build trust and create a safe exploration space.

Another vital component is to build trust and be vulnerable. It is no secret that sexual intimacy often involves being vulnerable with another person. For some people, they pretend as if they are strong and refuse to have their partner see them in a vulnerable state. During sex, vulnerability is most acceptable, and it is a time when trust plays a significant role in this process.

The recommendation is for persons to seek to engage in sexual activity; it must be with someone we can trust and feel emotionally safe with. Trusting your partner can enhance the overall experience and contribute to emotional well-being. Many of the issues that come from the whole emotional well-being connect to young people's body image and self-esteem.

As some might be aware, young people may struggle with body image and self-esteem, which can impact their emotional well-being during sexual encounters. It is important to remember that everyone is unique and beautiful in their own way, and even taking off one's clothes in front of another person is not the most straightforward task. Therefore, developing a positive body image and self-confidence can help reduce anxiety and enhance enjoyment during those intimate moments.

Such a thing called emotional connection is crucial to this conversation. Emotional connection in sexual intimacy refers to the deep bond and understanding established between two individuals during physical intimacy. It goes beyond the physical aspect of sex and involves a strong emotional attachment, trust, and vulnerability between the partners. This connection built open communication, empathy, and a shared intimacy and affection.

These are the grounds on which partners feel safe, secure, and deeply connected emotionally. Without this connection, the strength that fosters an intense and more satisfying sexual experience becomes rocky. Emotional connection in sexual intimacy can enhance pleasure while it creates a more profound sense of familiarity and strengthens the overall bond between the partners.

Sexual intimacy can deepen emotional connections between partners. When each person understands the emotional aspect of sex and that knowledge gained during that time, it goes beyond physical pleasure. This type of engagement is essential for this connection to be maintained.

Emotional connection can foster a sense of intimacy, trust, and satisfaction that contributes to overall emotional well-being. Sexual activity can evoke a wide range of emotions, as would have indicated before, both positive and negative. Young people need to understand that these emotions are normal and valid, and taking the time to process and reflect on these emotions can contribute holistically to growth and self-awareness.

It is also necessary to look critically at the after-sexual care. After engaging in sexual activities, many people feel ashamed and shy, with many emotions evoked. Nonetheless, it is crucial to prioritize self-care. Self-care includes practicing self-compassion and acknowledging and addressing any emotional concerns. Encouraging youths to understand their and their partners' emotions is vital. We need to remind them that it is okay to express their feelings and seek emotional support when needed. Emphasize the importance of consent, respect, and empathy to foster healthy emotional connections.

Online Safety And Healthy Boundaries:

Given the prevalence of online interactions, it is essential to discuss the potential risks associated with sexting, sharing explicit content, or engaging in online relationships. Young people should be educated about the importance of setting healthy digital boundaries, respecting others' privacy, and being cautious when sharing personal information. Encourage them to seek guidance from trusted adults if they encounter uncomfortable situations online.

Navigating sexual intimacy can be a transformative and beautiful experience for today's youths, but it requires knowledge, communication, and respect. By providing comprehensive guidance on consent, communication, safe sex practices, emotional well-being, and online safety, we can empower young individuals to cultivate healthy and fulfilling sexual relationships. Our collective responsibility is to ensure they have the necessary tools to embark on this journey with confidence, respect, and a deep understanding of themselves and their partners.

LESSON TWENTY-TWO

Exploring Sexuality And Religion, A Thoughtful Reflection

For many individuals, religion plays a significant role in shaping their beliefs, values, and moral perspectives. The interplay between sex and religion has been a topic of discussion for centuries, often marked by diverse interpretations and varying degrees of acceptance. This lesson aims to reflect thoughtfully on the subject, recognizing that opinions and practices differ across different religious traditions.

Sexuality And Religious Teachings:

Religious teachings often address human sexuality, guiding how people approach and express their sexual desires. Various religious texts offer different perspectives on premarital sex, contraception, homosexuality, and gender roles. These teachings are evident as an attempt to maintain moral standards, preserve family values, and foster community within religious frameworks.

Abstinence And Purity:

Many religious traditions emphasize abstinence, encouraging individuals to abstain from sexual activity until marriage. Purity is vital in religious contexts, emphasizing preserving a body for a committed and loving relationship. This perspective often promotes the idea that sex within the boundaries of marriage is not only permissible but also a sacred act that deepens the bond between partners.

While some religious communities adhere strictly to traditional teachings on sexuality, it is vital to recognize the diversity of interpretations within each faith. Individuals and groups may hold different views, influenced by cultural, historical, and personal factors, leading to various practices and stances on sexual matters.

Sexuality And LGBTQ+ Inclusion:

One area where religion and sexuality often turn into chaos is regarding LGBTQ+ individuals. Many religious traditions grapple with reconciling their teachings with the existence of diverse sexual orientations and gender identities. While some religious groups have embraced LGBTQ+ inclusion, others maintain a more conservative stance. This tension has sparked ongoing conversations about the intersectionality of faith, sexual orientation, and gender identity.

Health Approaches To Sexuality:

Regardless of religious beliefs, fostering healthy attitudes toward sexuality is crucial. Open dialogue, education, and consent-based approaches are paramount in promoting sexual well-being. Religious communities can be vital in providing support, guidance, and understanding for individuals navigating their sexual identities.

The Nexus between religion and sexuality is complex, and opinions may vary significantly within different religious traditions. It is essential to approach discussions on sex from a place of empathy and respect, recognizing the diversity of personal beliefs and experiences. Finding common ground in promoting healthy attitudes towards sexuality and fostering understanding can help bridge the gap between religious teachings and individual sexual expressions.

LESSON TWENTY-THREE

The Psychology Of Sex And Intimacy Essential To Human Existence

A man named Doctor Everton Carter lived in a quaint town in the bustling city of Chicago. He was a renowned psychologist known for his empathetic nature and deep understanding of the human mind. Driven by his insatiable curiosity, he dedicated his life to unravelling the complexities of human experience.

Doctor Carter firmly believed that sex and intimacy were fundamental aspects of human existence. He saw them not merely as physical acts but as powerful vehicles for emotional connection, self-discovery, and personal growth. With this conviction, he embarked on a journey to explore the depths of human sexuality and its impact on the psyche.

In his practice, Doctor Carter encountered individuals from all walks of life, each with unique stories and struggles. He listened intently, allowing his clients to express their deepest desires, fears, and vulnerabilities. Through his keen observations and understanding, he uncovered the intricate web of emotions woven within their experiences of intimacy. One fateful day, Doctor Carter was captivated by a young woman named Lily. Lily grappled with her understanding of intimacy, struggling to navigate the complexities of love and connection. As their sessions progressed, Doctor Carter realized that he too, was drawn towards Lily, not just as a patient but as a man awaiting his desires.

The boundaries between their professional relationship and personal connections blurred, challenging Doctor Carter's ethical principles. Yet he recognized an opportunity for profound exploration and growth for himself and Lily. Driven by his belief that personal experience informs professional understanding, he decided to embark on an intimate relationship with Lily but only after Lily's therapy.

Together, they embarked on a journey of self-discovery, using their shared experiences to delve deeper into the psyche. Doctor Carter encouraged Lily to express her desires, fears, and insecurities openly, creating an environment of trust and vulnerability. As they explored the intricacies of their physical connection, they began to uncover profound insights into their own emotions, thoughts, and beliefs.

Doctor Carter discovered that his role as a psychologist extended beyond the confines of his office. Through his encounters, he learned to analyze and express his feelings, emotions, and thoughts in ways he had never imagined. He realized that his understanding of intimacy was not limited to his academic knowledge but enriched by his experiences.

Their relationship, although unconventional, flourished. Doctor Carter and Lily learned to navigate the complexities of their desires while maintaining a deep respect for each other's boundaries and autonomy. Their journey together became a testament to the profound impact of intimacy and personal connection on one's emotional well-being.

Doctor Carter continued his work as a psychologist, armed with a newfound wisdom from his experiences. He recognized the importance of embracing our desires, acknowledging our vulnerabilities, and fostering meaningful connections. Through his insights and guidance, he helped countless others understand the profound role sex and intimacy play in the human experience.

Doctor Carter's legacy lived on as a respected psychologist and a man who dared to intertwine his professional pursuits with his personal growth. His story served as a reminder that sometimes, the most profound insights come from the mind, heart, and body.

For centuries, sex and intimacy have dominated on all levels, platforms, and spheres as they are integral aspects of our human experience. They have been influencing our physical, emotional, and psychological well-being. Beyond the primal instinct for procreation, these fundamental needs are essential in shaping our identities, relationships, and overall satisfaction with life. By examining the complex interplay between psychology and sexuality, we can better understand how these factors contribute to our existence.

The Evolutionary Perspective:

Sex and sexuality from the evolutionary standpoint, are primarily driven by the instinct to reproduce, ensuring the survival of our species. However, humans have evolved and, through the sexual experience, can now view sex beyond mere procreation but the incorporation of intimacy and pleasure. This idea suggests that the psychological aspect of sex is deeply rooted in our biology, serving as a mechanism to bond, feel pleasure, and enhance social connections.

The Power Of Intimacy:

Intimacy goes beyond the physical act of sex, encompassing emotional connection, vulnerability, and trust. It is a vital component of human relationships that, throughout human existence, provides a sense of belonging and fulfillment. People, in all their glory and magnificence, through their beautiful and wonderfully made bodies, have come in great control of great power.

The diversity of emotions accompanying intimacy puts the ones who recognize its absolute power at a tremendous advantage.

Intimate experiences release oxytocin, a hormone associated with bonding, attachment, and feelings of love. All these connections are the driving force that fosters emotional well-being, reducing stress, anxiety, and depression. Intimacy preserves exceptionally high levels of power for some unknown reason, where people make decisions outside of themselves and boundaries, especially when caught up in a physical movement. Women have done immeasurable acts of a profound sexual nature and used the power of intimacy to create all kinds of claims and firm hold on men.

The Psychological Benefits:

Psychology is essential in navigating sex and all its influence in our lives. Sexual activity is linked to numerous psychological benefits. It releases critical hormones: endorphins, dopamine, and serotonin, which contribute to feelings of happiness, relaxation, and overall well-being. Research reveals that regular sexual activity has improved self-esteem, body image, and satisfaction. Even outside of science, the physical feelings radiating from our minds and bodies can send off an aura of fulfillment and content that is evident to the naked eye. Moreover, intimate relationships offer emotional support, enhancing mental resilience and providing a sense of purpose.

The Impact Of Identity And Self-Expression:

Our identity shapes us through our associations, and sexuality plays a fundamental part in defining personal identity and self-expression. It is an avenue to explore the desires and preferences of someone, even within the confines of boundaries. When we understand and accept a person's sexual orientation and wishes, it therefore leads to increased self-acceptance, authenticity, and overall satisfaction with life. Moreover, healthy sexual expression can promote positive body image, self-confidence, and empowerment.

The Complex Influence Of Culture And Society:

With its abundance of cultural influence, society significantly impacts our attitudes, beliefs, and behaviours, especially concerning sex and intimacy. Societal norms, religious beliefs, and cultural practices shape our understanding of acceptable or taboo. As seen in many instances and amongst varying ethnic groups, these influences can facilitate healthy sexual expression or create barriers, leading to guilt, shame, or repression. Notwithstanding these variables, a greater understanding and our constant challenging of societal norms can promote greater sexual freedom, consent and choice, and equality for not just some but for all.

So, in concluding this chapter, it is safe to say that the psychology of sex and intimacy is a multifaceted and crucial aspect of human existence. It shapes and builds our relationships, self-perception, and overall well-being. Recognizing any intimacy's inherent biological, emotional, and psychological significance allows us to embrace healthy sexuality, foster meaningful connections, and ultimately lead more fulfilling lives. Therefore, there is a greater need to acknowledge and promote the importance of these aspects to create a more inclusive and understanding society where individuals can freely explore and express their sexuality.